CON

C000140129

FRENCH-ENGLISH
ENGLISH-FRENCH

Editor: ALAN S. LINDSEY

Illustrations by Valerie Naggs

HADLEY PAGER INFO

First published 1997 by Hadley Pager Info
ISBN 1-872739-05-9

Reprinted 2000

Printed and bound in Great Britain by Watkiss Studios Ltd.,
Biggleswade

Published by HADLEY PAGER INFO
Surrey House, 114 Tilt Road, Cobham, Surrey, KT11 3JH, England

EDITOR'S FOREWORD

It has given me great pleasure to edit Hadley's Conversational French Phrase Book, the content of which has been assembled from a wide variety of sources and now includes over two thousand phrases. These have been chosen to meet a wide range of conversational situations, but clearly it is impossible, within the confines of so small a volume, to cover every conversational gambit.

This Phrase Book should prove valuable to those with a working knowledge of French who wish to develop their conversational skills and achieve a greater command of the French language. It should meet the needs of students on exchange visits as well as those whose schooldays have passed. It differs from the more usual travel and shopping phrase book in that it embraces widely used conversational, colloquial and idiomatic phrases, and has the added advantage of eleven separate topic vocabularies covering words and phrases frequently used in conversations. A list of exclamations has also been included. Many of the phrases can readily be modified to meet the needs of a current conversation.

Phrases have been arranged alphabetically under keywords, but it should be noted that the French keyword may not always directly correspond with the keyword for the equivalent English phrase, particularly in the case of figurative phrases. Keywords are shown with their usual meanings attached and thereby also provide an aide-mémoire dictionary. Phrases marked with an asterisk are either slangy in content or are not recommended for use in formal conversation.

In conclusion I warmly thank Valerie Naggs for her contribution of amusing illustrations for the Phrase Book, and my wife Hazel for her considerable help and support in converting the idea of the Phrase Book into a practical reality.

Finally if you find that your favourite phrase has been overlooked, let me know (via the publisher), and it will be considered for inclusion in a later edition.

Alan Lindsey

CONTENTS

Abbreviations Used

abb	abbreviation	*f*	feminine noun
adj	adjective or	*m*	masculine noun
	adjectival phrase	*pl*	plural form
adv	adverb or	*prep*	preposition
	adverbial phrase	*pron*	pronoun
adj & adv	adjective and	*v*	verb
	adverb	*+inf*	with infinitive
conj	conjunction	*+vb*	with verb
excl	exclamation	*inv*	invariant

FRENCH-ENGLISH PHRASES

A

abattre v: to knock down, to drain, to demoralize

abattre de la besogne; abattre du travail — to get through a lot of work

elle est abattue par la chaleur — she is overcome by the heat

ne te laisse pas abattre — don't let things get you down (or demoralize you)

abord (d') m: first, at first

au premier abord; de prime abord — at first sight; initially

d'abord il ne connaissait personne — at first he didn't know anyone

dès le premier abord — from the outset; from the very first

abrégé m: summary

en abrégé — in brief; in a few words; in a nutshell

accepter v: to accept

accepter sans façon — to accept without fuss

accord m: agreement

d'accord! — O.K.!; agreed!

être d'accord avec — to agree with

se mettre d'accord sur — to agree on

tous sont tombés d'accord que — all agreed that

vous n'êtes pas d'accord? — don't you agree?

accorder (s') v: to agree, to grant

ils s'accordent comme chien et chat — they lead a cat and dog life

je vous l'accorde, j'avais tort — I agree (or grant) that I was wrong

accordés mpl: bride and groom

les accordés (ou les mariés) sont tout heureux — the bride and bridegroom are overjoyed

accueil m: welcome, reception

faire bon accueil à quelqu'un — to welcome someone; to make someone welcome

acheter v: to buy

acheter à prix d'or — to pay through the nose for

il a acheté chat en poche   *he has bought a pig in a poke*
il l'a acheté à crédit   *he bought it on credit*
je l'ai acheté d'occasion   *I bought it second-hand*

   achever *v:*   *to finish, to reach the end of*
j'ai achevé de me raser   *I have finished shaving*

   acquit *m:*   *receipt, release*
faire quelque chose par manière   *to do something as a matter*
d'acquit   *of form (or for form's sake)*

   acte *m:*   *act, deed, action*
dont acte   *duly noted*

   actualité *f:*   *current events, news*
discuter de l'actualité   *to discuss the latest news*
l'actualité sportive   *sports news*
les actualités télévisées sont à   *when is the television news?*
quelle heure?

   actuel,-elle *adj:*   *present, current, topical*
à l'heure actuelle   *at the present time*
dans le monde actuel on peut   *in the world of today one can*
trouver   *find*

   acuité *f:*   *acuteness, sharpness*
acuité visuelle; acuité de vision   *keeness of sight*

   adieu *m:*   *farewell, goodbye*
faire ses adieux à quelqu'un   *to say goodbye to someone*

   admettre *v:*   *to admit, to let in, to assume*
en admettant que   *granted that; assuming that;*
    supposing that

   admiration *f:*   *admiration*
elle fait l'admiration de tous   *she is admired by everyone*

   adorer *v:*   *to adore*
j'adore le millefeuille   *I love cream and custard*
    pastry

   adresser *v:*   *to address*
adresser une prière à Dieu   *to offer up a prayer to God*

   adresser (se) *v:*   *to apply*
s'adresser à qui de droit   *to apply to the proper person*
    (or quarter)

   advenir *v:*   *to come to pass, to occur*
advienne que pourra   *come what may*

   affaire *f:*   *affair, matter, business*
c'est l'affaire d'une minute   *it will only take a minute*

c'est mon affaire, non la tienne	it's my business, not yours
c'est une affaire du cœur	it is a love affair
en voilà une affaire	here's a pretty kettle of fish
l'affaire est dans le sac	it's in the bag; the deal is all sewn up
se tirer d'affaire	to get out of a difficulty; to get out of trouble
son affaire est faite!	his number is up!

affection *f:* affection

payer de retour l'affection de quelqu'un	to return someone's affection

affirmer *v:* to maintain, to assert

affirmer avec force	to insist; to state firmly
pouvez-vous l'affirme?	can you be certain about it?; can you swear to it?

affût *m:* hide, hiding-place

être à l'affût de quelque chose	to be on the look out for something

agacer *v:* to set on edge, to jar

cela m'agace les dents	that sets my teeth on edge

âge *m:* age

à la fleur de l'âge	at the prime of life; in one's prime
accuser son âge	to look one's age; to show one's age
d'un certain âge	oldish; getting on; middle-aged
entre deux âges	middle-aged
il est arrivé à son troisième âge	he is in retirement; he has become a senior citizen
il est d'âge à se conduire	he is old enough to look after himself
l'âge ingrat	the awkward age; the difficult age

agir *v:* to act, to behave

agir en dessous	to act underhandedly
agir en tout bien tout honneur	to act with only the most honourable intentions
il s'agit de	it's a matter of; it's a question of

7

aguets (aux) *mpl:* watchful, on the watch

avoir l'oreille aux aguets   to keep one's ears open

aïeux *mpl:* forefathers, forebears

mes aïeux   my forebears; my grand-
parents

aigre *adj:* sour

tourner à l'aigre (ou au vinaigre)   to turn sour

aigrir *v:* to embitter, to sour

être aigri   to have a chip on one's
shoulder

aimable *adj:* kind

c'est très aimable (ou gentil)
à vous   that is very kind of you

aimer *v:* to like, to love

aimer à la folie   to be crazy about; to love to
distraction

aimer autant   would just as soon; be just as
well; may as well

aimer la table   to like good food; to be fond
of good living

aimer mieux (+inf)   would rather; would sooner;
would prefer to

ainsi *adv:* thus, so, in this way

ainsi va la monde   that's the way of the world

ainsi que   just as; as well as

et c'est ainsi que   and it is in this way that

s'il en est ainsi, je m'en vais   if that (or such) is the case,
I'm leaving

air *m:* air, atmosphere, look

avoir un air de sainte nitouche   to look so very innocent

ça m'a l'air d'un mensonge   it sounds to me like a lie

donner de l'air à une chambre   to air a room

elle a l'air aisé   she has an easy manner

prendre un air entendu   to put on a knowing look

aise *f:* joy, comfort, satisfaction, ease

être à son aise; être à l'aise   to be (or feel) at ease; to be
comfortable; to be well-off

être mal à l'aise (ou peu à l'aise)   to be (or feel) ill at ease; to
be uneasy

se mettre à son aise	*to make oneself comfortable; to make oneself at home*
aller (s'en) *v: to go away*	
allez-vous en, vous me dérangez!	*go away, you're disturbing me!*
aller *v: to go*	
aller à la dérive	*to go to pot; to go to the dogs*
aller à un train d'enfer	*to go at a furious rate; to go flat out*
aller à vau-l'eau	*to go to rack and ruin; to be on the road to ruin; to be falling apart*
aller de mal en pis	*to go from bad to worse*
aller et venir	*to walk up and down; to walk about*
aller (ou marcher) clopin-clopant	*to limp along; to hobble along*
aller son (petit) train	*to go along at one's own pace*
allez trouver le patron pour cette question	*go and see the boss about this question*
cela va de soi	*it goes without saying; it's self-evident*
il y est allé carrément	*he made no bones about it; he went bluntly to the point*
il y va de trente francs	*it's a matter of thirty francs; it's a question of thirty francs*
n'y va pas quatre chemins!	*give it to me straight!; don't beat about the bush!*
y aller par quatre chemins	*to beat around the bush*
allusion *f: hint*	
faire une allusion	*to drop a hint*
amabilité *f: kindness*	
il a eu l'amabilité de dire	*he was kind enough to say*
ambiguïté *f: ambiguity*	
parler sans ambiguïté; parler sans détours	*to speak plainly*
âme *f: soul*	
comme une âme en peine	*like a lost soul*

ancien

   amende *f:* fine, apology

faire amende honorable   *to make amends; to make a*
full apology

   amener *v:* to bring, to bring about

j'ai amené la conversation sur   *I brought the conversation*
un autre sujet   *round to another subject*

   ami *m,* **amie** *f:* friend

ils sont amis (ou copains)   *they're as thick as thieves*
comme cochons

   amiable *adj:* amicable

régler une affaire à l'amiable   *to settle a difference out of*
court

   amitié *f:* friendship

se lier d'amitié avec quelqu'un   *to make friends with*
someone

prendre quelqu'un en amitié   *to befriend someone;*
to take a liking to someone

une amitié de courte durée   *a short (or short-lived)*
friendship

   amont (en) *m:* upstream

le pont est en amont d'ici   *the bridge is upstream from*
here

   amoureux: *m & adj,* **amoureuse** *f & adj:* lover, sweetheart

être amoureux de   *to be in love with;*
to be enamoured with

tomber amoureux de   *to fall in love with*
tomber amoureux fou   *to fall head over heels in love*

   amuser (s') *v:* to play, to have a good time, to enjoy oneself

est-ce que tu t'es bien amusé   *did you enjoy yourself in*
à Nice?   *Nice?*

nous nous sommes bien amusés   *we had a great time; we had*
great fun

s'amuser à faire   *to have fun doing; to enjoy*
oneself doing

   ancien(ne) *m, f:* ancient, antique, old flame

faire (dans) l'ancien   *to be in the antique trade;*
to sell antiques

rencontrer un(e) ancien(ne)   *to meet by chance an old*
flame

âne *m: donkey, ass*
être comme l'âne de Buridan — *to be unable to make up one's mind*

ange *m: angel*
être aux anges — *to be delighted; to be in the seventh heaven*

année *f: year*
il va à la pêche toute l'année — *he goes fishing all the year round*

bonne année! — *Happy New Year!*

annonce *f: advertisement*
vous avez essayé les petites annonces? — *you've tried the small ads? (or classified advertisements?)*

annoncer *v: to announce*
annoncer à tous les échos — *to tell all and sundry; to cry from the rooftops*

apparence *f: appearance*
contre toute apparence — *against all expectations*
en apparence — *apparently; seemingly; on the face of it*

selon toute apparence — *to all appearances; in all probability*

appartenir *v: to belong*
pour des raisons qui m'appartiennent — *for my own reasons*

appel *m: call, appeal*
faire l'appel — *to call the roll; to call out the names*

faire appel à — *to appeal to; to call on; to require*

appeler *v: to call, to telephone*
appeler au secours — *to call for help*
appeler un chat un chat — *to call a spade a spade*
il faut appeler le docteur — *we must call the doctor*

apprendre *v: to learn, to teach, to tell*
apprendre à vivre à quelqu'un — *to teach someone a lesson; to sort someone out*

apprendre quelque chose par cœur — *to learn something by heart*

11

arriver

j'ai appris à Julien la nouvelle	I have told Julian the news

appui m: *support*

à l'appui (de)	in support of this; to back this up

après prep: *after*

d'après lui (ou elle)	according to him (or her); in his (or her) opinion
l'instant d'après il était parti	the next moment he was gone

argent m: *money, silver*

en avoir pour son argent	to get one's money's worth

arracher v: *to dig up, to extract, to pull*

on se l'arrache	he (or she, or it) is all the rage

arranger v: *to arrange, to settle*

arranger les choses	to put things straight; to sort things out
cela m'arrange bien	that suits me nicely; that's fine by me
cela n'arrange rien	that doesn't help anything
s'arranger avec quelqu'un	to come to an agreement with someone
s'arranger de	to make do with; to put up with

arrière-pensée f: *ulterior motive, reservation*

sans arrière-pensée	without reserve

arriver v: *to arrive, to happen, to reach*

arriver à destination	to reach one's journey's end
arriver dans un fauteuil	to win hands down; to romp home
arriver en coup de vent	to burst in; to breeze in; to arrive at full speed
cela arrive comme marée en carême	this comes just at the right time
cela arrivera comme mars en carême	it's bound to happen
cela peut arriver à n'importe qui	it could happen to anyone
c'est arrivé hier	it happened yesterday
en arriver là	to come to this

arroser *v:* to water, to drink to

cela s'arrose! — that calls for a drink!

article *m:* item, stock item, article

faire l'article — to boost; to push; to sing the praises of

assez *adj & adv:* enough

assez parlé, des actes! — enough said, let's have some action!

cela suffit, merci; c'est assez; merci — that's enough thank you

c'est assez!; c'en est assez!; en voilà assez! — I've had enough!; enough is enough!

assiette *f:* plate

il n'est pas dans son assiette — he is out of sorts; he's a bit off-colour

assommer *v:* to stun, to overwhelm, to bore

assommer quelqu'un avec des fleurs — to damn someone with faint praise

assortir *v:* to match

les époux sont mal assortis — they are an ill-matched couple

attacher *v:* to tie, to attach

s'attacher aux pas de — to dog the steps of; to follow closely

attaque *f:* attack, onset

elle est toujours d'attaque — she is still going strong

ne pas se sentir d'attaque — not to feel up to it; to feel off form

d'attaque — on form; in top form

attendre *v:* to await, to wait for, to expect

attendre les événements — to await events; to sit tight

attendre un bébé; attendre un enfant — to be expecting (a baby)

cela valait la peine d'attendre — that was worth waiting for

en attendant — meanwhile; in the meantime; all the same

en attendant qu'il vienne, nous jouions aux cartes — while waiting for him to come we played cards

il va falloir attendre; il va falloir voir venir — we'll just have to wait and see

s'attendre à quelque chose — to expect something

13

attente *f:* waiting, expectation

contre toute attente — quite unexpectedly; contrary to expectation

attirer *v:* to attract

s'attirer des ennuis — to get into a mess; to bring trouble on oneself

attraper *v:* to catch

attraper le coup; attraper le tour de main — to get the hang (or knack) of something

cette maladie s'attrape facilement — this disease is catching

j'ai attrapé un rhume — I've caught a cold

aube *f:* dawn, daybreak

à l'aube; dès l'aube — at dawn; at first light; at daybreak

aucun,-e *adj:* no, not any

aucun autre — no one else

au delà *adv:* beyond

au delà de la rivière — beyond the river

auparavant *adv:* beforehand, previously

deux mois auparavant — two months before; two months earlier

quelques instants auparavant — just previously

auprès de *prep:* next to, compared with

il restait auprès de sa femme — he stayed near (or close to) his wife

mon salaire est élevé auprès du leur — my pay is high compared with theirs

aussitôt *adv:* straight away, immediately

aussitôt dit, aussitôt fait — no sooner said than done

aussitôt que possible; dans le délai le plus bref — as soon as possible

aussitôt que vous le pourrez — at your earliest convenience

autant *adv:* as much, so much, as many, so many

autant parler à un mur — one might as well be talking to a wall

autant que possible — as much as possible; as far as possible

autant que je m'en souvienne — to the best of my recollection

autant que je sache	*as far as I know; to the best of my knowledge*
autant vaudrait dire que	*one might as well say that*
d'autant plus	*all the more*
d'autant que; d'autant plus que	*all the more so since (or because)*
d'autant moins	*all the less; even less*
en faire autant	*to follow suit; to do the same*
encore autant	*as much again*
le temps sera augmenté d'autant	*the time will be increased accordingly*
pour autant	*for all that*

autrement dit

autrement *adv:* *differently, otherwise*

il faut s'y prendre tout autrement	*we'll have to go about it quite differently*

autres *pron:* *others*

nous autres	*the like of us; we (emph)*

aval (en) *m:* *downstream*

l'écluse est en aval d'ici	*the lock is downstream*

avaler *v:* *to swallow*

avaler des couleuvres	*to swallow insults; to be taken in*
avaler le morceau	*to swallow a bitter pill; to bite the bullet*
l'avaler d'un trait; l'avaler d'un seul coup	*to swallow it in one gulp; to drink it in one go*

avancer *v:* *to advance, to move forward*

à quoi cela m'avance-t-il?	*what good does that do me?*
avancer au même rythme que	*to keep pace with*
avancer par saccades	*to move forward in fits and starts*
il n'en est pas plus avancé	*he's no better off; he's no further on*
votre montre avance de cinq minutes	*your watch is five minutes fast*

avant *prep:* *before*

avant peu	*before long; shortly*

avant (en) *adv:* *forward*

en avant la musique!	*off we go!; strike up the band!*

avant de *conj:* before
avant de venir vous voir — *before coming to see you*

avant-dernier *m*, **avant-dernière** *f:* next to last
il est l'avant-dernier — *he is the last but one*

avantage *m:* advantage
avoir un avantage sur quelqu'un — *to have an advantage over someone*

avantageux,-euse *adj:* worthwhile, conceited
il est un homme avantageux — *he is a conceited man; he is a presuming fellow*

avenant,-e *adj:* pleasant, pleasing
il a de manières avenantes — *he has pleasing manners; he has engaging manners*

avenir *m:* future
à l'avenir — *in future; from now on*
assurer l'avenir de quelqu'un — *to make provision for someone's future*
un homme d'avenir — *an up-and-coming man; a man with a future*

avis *m:* advice, notice, opinion
à mon avis — *in my opinion*
avis aux amateurs, je vends mon vélo! — *anybody interested? I'm selling my bicycle!*
être d'avis de faire quelque chose — *to be in favour of doing something*
sauf avis contraire — *unless one hears to the contrary*

aviser *v:* to advise
bien/mal avisé — *well/ill advised*

avoine *f:* oat(s)
semer sa folle avoine — *to sow one's wild oats*

avoir *v:* to have
avoir ce qu'il faut — *to have what it takes*
en avoir assez; en avoir marre — *to be fed up; to be cheesed off*
en avoir contre; avoir une dent contre — *to have it in for*
il se fait facilement avoir — *he's easily taken in*
quoi qu'il en ait — *no matter what he may think*

avouer *v:* to confess, to admit
s'avouer coupable   to admit one's guilt

B

bagatelle *f:* trinket, knick-knack
être porté sur la bagatelle   to have sex on the mind; to
           be a randy so-and-so

baigner *v:* to bath, to bathe
ça baigne!; tout baigne!   everything is fine!; really
           super-duper!
ça baigne dans l'huile   things are running smoothly;
           everything is looking great

bain *m:* bath, swim
être dans le bain   to be in the know; to know
           the ropes
mettre quelqu'un dans le bain   to put someone in the
           picture; to incriminate
           someone

baisser *v:* to lower, to turn down, to dwindle
le jour baisse   darkness is approaching; the
           light is failing

banqueroute *f:* bankruptcy
faire banqueroute   to go bankrupt

barbe *f:* beard
faire quelque chose à la barbe   to do something under
de quelqu'un   someone's nose
quelle barbe!   what a nuisance!; what a
           drag!

bas (en) *m:* downstairs, down below
il habite en bas (en haut)   he lives downstairs (upstairs)

bas, basse *adj:* low
au bas mot   at the very least; at the
           lowest estimate
être au plus bas   to be very low; to be at a low
           ebb

base *f:* base, basis
à base de   composed (mainly) of; based

bâtir *v:* to build

bâtir (ou faire) des châteaux en Espagne — to build castles in the air; to build castles in Spain

bâton *m:* stick, staff

elle est mon bâton de vieillesse — she is my prop in old age

il a son bâton de maréchal — he has risen as far as he can

mettre des bâtons dans les roues — to put a spoke in some one's wheel; to put a spanner in the works

battre *v:* to beat, to strike

battre à plate couture — to beat hollow; to beat hands down

battre de l'aile — to be flustered; to be exhausted; to be on one's last legs

battre en breche une théorie — to demolish a theory; to assail a theory

battre froid à quelqu'un — to be cool towards someone; to cold-shoulder someone

battre la breloque (appareil) — to be on the blink; to be giving out

battre la campagne — to be delirious

battre le pavé — to walk the streets; to wander aimlessly about

battre quelqu'un à son propre jeu — to beat someone at his own game

il ferait battre des montagnes — he's a troublemaker

je m'en bats l'œil — I don't care a rap!; I don't care a damn!

soirée qui bat son plein — party in full swing; party at its height

bavard *adj:* talkative, garrulous

il est bavard comme une pie — he'll talk your ear off; he's a windbag

baver *v:* to slobber, to drool

en baver d'admiration — to gasp in admiration

en baver — to have a rough time of it; to have a hard time

bavure *f:* hitch, flaw, unfortunate mistake

c'est net et sans bavure! — it's absolutely clear!

sans bavure	flawless; perfect
bayer *v:* to stand gaping	
bayer aux corneilles	to stand gaping; to star gaze
beau, bel, belle *adj:* beautiful, lovely	
avoir beau jeu de	to have every opportunity to
ávoir le beau rôle	to come off best (in a situation); to show oneself in a good light; to have the limelight
c'est un beau brin de fille; c'est une jolie fille	she's a good looker
être dans de beaux draps	to be in a fix (or fine mess)
faire le beau	to sit up and beg (dog); to curry favour
il est beau gosse; c'est un beau gars	he's a good looker
il s'est bel et bien trompé	he got it well and truly wrong
il y a belle lurette de cela	that was a long, long while ago; that was donkey's years ago
se faire beau; se faire belle	to get dressed up; to get spruced up
beaucoup *adv:* much, many	
à beaucoup près	far from it
de beaucoup	by a long way; by far; far and away
il y est pour beaucoup	to a large extent he's responsible for it
bec *m:* beak	
tomber sur un bec	to hit a snag; to run into a difficulty; to be stymied
béer *v:* to be (wide) open	
je suis resté bouche bée d'étonnement	I stood gaping with astonishment
besogne *f:* work, job	
aller trop vite en besogne	to be slapdash; to be too quick off the mark
besoin *m:* need, want	
au besoin	if need be; if necessary

avoir besoin de quelque chose	*to need something; to be in need of something*
en cas de besoin	*if the need arises; in case of necessity*
est-il besoin de vous dire?	*need I tell you?*
faire ses besoins	*to relieve oneself; to spend a penny*
pour les besoins de la cause	*for the purpose in hand*

bête *f & adj:* beast, fool, stupid, foolish

ce n'est pas possible d'être aussi bête!	*how can anyone be so stupid!*
ce n'est pas bête!	*that's not a bad suggestion (or idea)*
c'est bête comme chou	*it's as easy as pie; it's dead simple*
c'est ma bête noire	*that is my pet aversion (or pet hate)*
être bête comme ses pieds	*to be a stupid fool; to be as thick as a plank*
faire la bête	*to act silly; to behave foolishly*
il est bête à manger du foin	*he is a downright fool (or ass)*
je me suis vraiment senti bête	*I felt such a fool*
pas si bête!	*not if I can help it!*
que je suis bête!	*how stupid of me!; what a fool I am!*

bêtise *f:* stupidity, foolishness

dépenser tout son argent en bêtises	*to fritter away one's money*
faire des bêtises	*to play the fool; to make blunders; to get into mischief; to do stupid things*
quelle bêtise!	*what nonsense!*

beurre *m:* butter

ça fait mon beurre	*it's the very thing for me*
c'est du beurre; c'est un vrai beurre	*it's a pushover; it's as easy as wink*
faire son beurre	*to make one's pile; to feather one's nest*

vouloir le beurre et l'argent du beurre	to want to have one's cake and eat it

bien *adj & adv:* well, good

aller bien	to be well; to be right (clock)
bel et bien	altogether; well and truly
bien en chair	plump; well-padded (person)
bien entendu; bien sûr; bien évidemment	of course
c'est bien fait pour lui	it serves him right
ce n'est pas bien sorcier	there's really nothing to it; it's easy
être bien avec quelqu'un	to be on good terms with someone
il s'y prend bien	he goes the right way about it
un changement en bien (ou en mieux)	a change for the better

bien *m:* good person, possession, property

avoir du bien au soleil	to own land
des gens de bien	good people; well-to-do people
un homme de bien	a good man; a wealthy man; a man of property

bien-être *m:* well-being, comfort

un grand sentiment de bien-être	a great feeling of well-being

bientôt *adv:* soon

à bientôt!	see you soon!

bière *f:* beer

ce n'est pas de la petite bière	it's not to be sneezed at

blaguer *v:* to be joking, to tease

il a dû le dire en blaguant	he must have said that tongue in cheek

blanc *adj & m:* white

aller (ou passer) du blanc au noir	to go from one extreme to another
devenir blanc comme un linge	to become as white as a sheet

blesser *v:* to hurt, to injure, to wound

blesser au vif	to cut to the quick
c'est là où le bât le blesse	that's where the shoe pinches

21

bonnet

    bleu *m:* blue

être un bleu	to be a greenhorn; to be a beginner
il m'en a fait voir de bleues	he has led me a fine dance
il n'y a vu que du bleu	he didn't twig; he didn't smell a rat
j'en suis resté bleu	I was flabbergasted

    boire *v:* to drink

boire à grandes gorgées	to drink greedily; to gulp down
boire à petites gorgées; boire à petits coups	to sip
boire à tire-larigot	to drink like a fish
boire du petit lait	to lap it up (praise); to feel pleased with oneself
boire en Suisse	to drink by oneself; to be a solitary drinker
boire sur le zinc	to drink at the bar
boire un bouillon	to go under; to be ruined; to make a big loss
boire une coup; boire un verre	to have a drink
ce n'est pas la mer à boire	it is not so very difficult
il sait boire!	he can hold his liquor!
il y a à boire et à manger là-dedans	it has its good and its bad points; you have to take it with a grain of salt

    bon, bonne *adj:* good

il est parti pour tout de bon	he's gone for good

    bondir *v:* to jump, to leap, to bounce

faire bondir quelqu'un	to make someone hopping mad

    bonheur *m:* happiness

par bonheur	fortunately; luckily

    bonnet *m:* bonnet, hat, cap

c'est bonnet blanc et blanc bonnet	it comes to the same thing; it's six of one and half a dozen of the other
ce sont deux têtes sous le même bonnet	they are alike in everything; they are as thick as thieves

un gros bonnet	VIP; Very Important Person; a big shot
bonté f: kindness, goodness	
ayez la bonté de	have the kindness to
bosse f: hump, bump	
avoir la bosse de quelque chose	to have a flair for something; to have a gift for something
botte f: boot	
en avoir plein les bottes	to have had it up to here; to be fed up to the back teeth
botter v: to put boots on	
ça me botte	I like that; I fancy that; that suits me down to the ground
bouc m: goat	
être le bouc émissaire	to be the scapegoat
bouche f: mouth	
bouche cousue!	mum's the word!; don't breathe a word!; close-lipped
faire de bouche à bouche à quelqu'un	to give someone the kiss of life; to give mouth to mouth resuscitation
passer de bouche en bouche	to pass by word of mouth; to be rumoured about
bouchée f: mouthful	
mettre les bouchées doubles	to get cracking; to get stuck in
ne faire qu'une bouchée de (un plat, adversaire)	to make short work of (a dish, opponent)
bourrique f: donkey, pigheaded person	
faire tourner quelqu'un en bourrique	to drive someone round the bend (or up the wall)
bousculer v: to jostle, to shove	
ça se bouscule au portillon	he can't get his words out fast enough
bout m: end	
au bout du compte	after all; in the final analysis
être au bout de son latin; être au bout (de son rouleau)	to be at the end of one's tether; to be at one's wits' end

ça

bouteille *f:* bottle
prendre de la bouteille*

to be getting on in years; to
be older and wiser

bras *m:* arm
bras dessus, bras dessous
les bras m'en tombent

arm in arm
I'm thunderstruck; I'm
flabbergasted

brave *adj & m:* brave, bold
c'est un brave type
c'est un homme brave
faire le brave

he's a decent sort (or fellow)
he's a brave man
to put on a bold front; to
swagger

brèche *f:* gap, breach
être sur la brèche

to be hard at it

bredouille *adj:* empty-handed
il est rentré (ou revenu)
bredouille

he returned (home) empty-
handed

briller *v:* to shine, to sparkle
briller par son absence

to be conspicuous by one's
absence

bruit *m:* noise, rumour
le bruit court que

it is reported that; rumour has
it that

un bruit à vous fendre la tête
(ou les oreilles)

an excruciating noise; an
ear-splitting noise

but *m:* aim, goal, objective
aller droit au but
dans ce but

to go straight to the point
for that (or this) purpose;
with this aim in view

de but en blanc
quel est le but de sa visite?

point-blank; bluntly; suddenly
what is the purpose of his (or
her) visit?

C

ça (= **cela**) *pron:* that, it
çà et là

here and there; this way and
that way

c'est ça
et avec ça!

that's right; that's it
nonsense!; you're joking!

et avec ça, madame? — *anything else madam? (in shop)*

cacher *v:* to hide
cacher le jour à quelqu'un — *to stand in someone's light*

cafard *m:* cockroach, melancholy
avoir le cafard — *to have the blues; to be down in the dumps*

calé,-e *adj:* bright, clever
il est très calé en football — *he's pretty hot at football*

carotte *f:* carrot
les carottes sont cuites! — *they've had it!; it's all over for us!*

tirer une carotte de longueur à quelqu'un — *to pitch someone a long yarn*

carotter *v:* to nick, to pinch, to fiddle, to cheat
carotter le service — *to shirk duty; to malinger*
elle carotte sur l'argent des commissions — *she fiddles the housekeeping money*
il essaie toujours de carotter — *he is always trying to fiddle a bit for himself*

carrière *f:* career, course
donner libre carrière (ou cours) à — *to give full play to; to give free rein to*

cas *m:* case, situation
c'est le cas ou jamais — *it's now or never*
en cas de besoin — *in case of need; if need be*
en pareil cas — *in such a case*
en tout cas — *at all events; at any rate; anyway*

faire grand cas de — *to value highly; to have a high opinion of*

le cas échéant — *if the case arises; if need be*

casse-cou *m, f, inv:* daredevil, reckless person
mon frère est un casse-cou — *my brother is a reckless fellow*

casser *v:* to break
casser les pieds à quelqu'un — *to bore someone stiff; to wear someone out; to get on someone's nerves*

il me casse les pieds — *he's an absolute pest; he's a pain in the neck*

se casser la tête — *to rack one's brains*

se casser le nez — *to come unstuck; to come a cropper; to find nobody in*

cause *f:* cause

à cause de — *on account of; because of; owing to*

causer *v:* to chat, to talk

causer travail (ou politique) — *to talk shop (or politics)*

(c'est) assez causé! — *enough said, let's get down to business!*

cérémonie *f:* ceremony

il fait des cérémonies — *he stands on ceremony*

chair *f:* flesh

ce n'est ni chair ni poisson — *to be neither flesh, fowl nor good red herring*

en chair et en os — *in the flesh; as large as life*

j'en ai la chair de poule — *it makes my flesh creep; it gives me goose pimples*

chance *f:* luck

bonne chance! — *good luck!*

courir la chance — *to take one's chance; to try one's luck*

par un coup de chance; par un coup de veine — *as luck would have it; by a stroke of luck*

quelle chance! — *what luck!; how lucky!*

vous avez de la chance; tu a de la chance — *you're lucky*

change *m:* exchange

donner le change à quelqu'un — *to put someone off the scent (or track)*

changer *v:* to change

cela change tout! — *that changes everything; that makes all the difference*

changer d'avis; changer d'idée — *to change one's mind (or opinion)*

il faut changer de conduite — *you must turn over a new leaf; you must mend your ways*

chanson *f:* song

ça, c'est une autre chanson — that's quite a different matter; that's quite a different story

je connais la chanson (ou la musique) — I've heard it all before

chanter *v:* to sing

ça ne me chante pas — I'm not keen on the idea

chanter toujours la même antienne — to harp on the same old theme

ils chantaient à qui mieux mieux — they all sang their best

chapeau *m* **de roue:** hub cap (car)

démarrer sur les chapeaux de roue — to shoot off at high speed; to take off like a shot

charbon *m:* coal

aller au charbon — to get down to (hard) work

charger *v:* to load, burden

j'ai passé une semaine chargée — I have had a busy week

charger (se) *v:* to see to, to take care of

je m'en chargerai — I will see to it

charmant,-e *adj:* charming

c'est un collaborateur charmant — he is a charming man to work with

elle est plus charmante que jamais — she is more charming than ever

charrue *f:* plough

mettre la charrue devant les bœufs — to put the cart before the horse

chasser *v:* to hunt, to shoot

chasser de race — to be a chip off the old block; to run in the family

chat *m:* cat

avoir un chat dans la gorge — to have a frog in one's throat

il n'y a pas de quoi fouetter un chat — there's nothing to make a fuss about

il n'y avait pas un chat dedans — there wasn't a soul inside

j'ai autre chats à fouetter — I have other fish to fry; I have more important things to do

chaud *adj:* warm, hot

on a eu chaud — it was a close call

chaussure *f:* shoe

mes chaussures prennent l'eau — *my shoes let in water*

chemin *m:* path, lane, track

elle est revenue par le même chemin — *she returned the same way*

être en chemin de faire quelque chose — *to be well on the way to achieving something*

j'ai pris un chemin de traverse — *I took a short cut; I took a path across the fields*

chemise *f:* shirt

en manches (ou bras) de chemise — *in one's shirt-sleeves*

chercher *v:* to look for, to search, to seek

chercher la petite bête — *to split hairs; to quibble*

chercher midi à quatorze heures — *to look for difficulties; to look for complications; to complicate the issue*

chercher une aiguille dans une botte de foin — *to look for a needle in a haystack*

cheval *m:* horse

monter à cheval; faire du cheval — *to ride a horse*

savez-vous monter à cheval? — *can you ride (a horse)?*

cheveu *m,* **cheveux** *mpl:* hair

arriver comme un cheveu sur la soupe — *to be inopportune; to be out of place; to happen at the most awkward moment*

elle a les cheveux en bataille — *her hair was dishevelled*

se faire des cheveux — *to worry; to worry oneself grey; to fret*

chez *prep:* home, house

passer chez quelqu'un — *to call on someone*

chien *m:* dog

entre chien et loup; au crépuscule — *at dusk; in the twilight*

chiffre *m:* figure, numeral, sum

en chiffres connus — *in plain figures*

chœur *m:* choir, chorus

un enfant de chœur — *a naïve and innocent person*

chose *f:* thing

ne pas faire les choses à demi — *not to do things by halves*

chute *f:* fall
faire une chute — *to have a fall*
ciel *m:* sky, heaven
il est au septième ciel — *he's in the seventh heaven; he's on cloud nine*

clair,-e *adj:* clear
avoir un esprit clair — *to be a clear thinker*
claquer *v:* to bang, to flap
(faire) claquer la porte — *to slam the door; to walk out in a huff*

clef, clé *f:* key
mettre sous clef — *to put under lock and key*
mettre la clef sous la porte — *to shut up shop; to do a bunk; to clear out*

cœur *m:* heart
apprendre par cœur — *to learn by heart*
avoir le cœur sur la main — *to be open-handed; to be big hearted*
avoir le cœur sur les lèvres — *to be open-hearted*
il y va tout son cœur — *he does his utmost*
je veux en avoir le cœur net — *I want to be clear in my own mind about it; I want to get to the bottom of it*
prendre quelque chose à cœur — *to take something to heart*
un dur au cœur tendre — *someone whose bark is worse than their bite*

coiffer (se) *v:* to do one's hair, to put on (hat)
être né coiffé — *to be born lucky*
elle est toujours bien/mal coiffé — *she always has well-kept/ untidy hair*
se faire coiffer au poteau — *to get beaten at the post*
coincer *v:* to catch out, to stymie
je suis coincé; je suis dans une impasse — *I'm stymied*
colère *f:* anger
être hors de soi en colère — *to be beside onself with anger*

comble *m:* heaped measure
pour comble de malheur — *to make matters worse; to crown everything*

29

comme *conj:* as, like

c'était amusant comme tout — *it was terribly funny*

comme ci comme ça; — *so-so; fair to middling*
couci-couça

comment *adv:* how

comment ça se fait? — *how come?; how is it?*

comment donc? — *how do you mean?*

comment se fait-il qu'il soit — *how is it that he has gone?*
parti?

compliment *m:* compliment, (pl) congratulations

mes compliments!; toutes mes — *congratulations!*
félicitations!

compris,-e *adj:* inclusive, including

y compris; compris; inclus — *inclusive; including; included*

compte *m:* account, count

acheter à bon compte — *to buy at a cheap rate; to buy*
cheap

tenir compte de — *to take into account*

compter *v:* to count

sans compter — *not to mention; not counting*

concerner *v:* to concern, to affect

en ce qui me concerne — *as far as I am concerned*

concurrence *f:* concurrence

jusqu'à concurrence de — *to the amount of; not*
exceeding; to the extent of

condition *f:* condition, requirement

à condition; sous condition; — *on approval*
à l'essai

conduire *v:* to lead, to manage, to drive (vehicle)

bien conduire (ou mener) sa — *to manage one's affairs well*
barque

confiance *f:* confidence, trust

ça, vous pouvez me faire — *you can rely on me for that*
confiance

congé *m:* holiday, leave, time off

prendre congé de quelqu'un — *to take leave of someone*

prendre un congé d'une semaine — *to take a week off; to take a*
week's leave

30

connaissance *f*: knowledge, acquaintance, consciousness

faire connaissance avec	to become acquainted with; to obtain knowledge of
il parle en connaissance de cause	he knows what he is talking about; he has full knowledge of the facts
lier connaissance avec quelqu'un	to strike up an acquaintance with someone
perdre/reprendre connaissance	to lose/regain consciousness

connaître *v*: to know, to be acquainted with

connaître la musique	to know the score
connaître les faits sur le bout du doigt	to have the facts at one's fingertips
connaître les ficelles	to know the ropes
en connaître un bout	to know a thing or two
en connaître un rayon	to know it inside out; to be really clued up about it
être connu sous le nom de	to be known by the name of
il connait tous les dessous	he has inside information
il se connait parfaitement en vins	he is an expert judge of wines
je le connais de nom	I know him by name
je le connais de vue	I know him by sight

conscience *f*: awareness, conscience, consciousness

en toute sûreté de conscience	with a clear conscience

conseil *m*: advice, counsel

j'ai besoin d'un conseil au sujet de	I need some advice on
je voudrais vous demander conseil	I would like some advice

conseiller *v*: to recommend, to advise

il est conseillé de	it is advisable to

considérer *v*: to consider

tout bien considéré	all things considered; on the whole

consigné,-e *adj*: returnable

non consigné	non-returnable

contenance *f*: countenance, composure, attitude

faire bonne contenance	to put on a bold (or brave) face

coup

je lui ai fait perdre contenance	I stared him out of countenance

contre *prep:* against

par contre	on the contrary; on the other hand

contrecœur (à) *adv:* reluctantly, unwillingly

il l'a fait, mais à contrecœur	he did it, but reluctantly

convalescence *f:* convalescence

entrer en convalescence	to become convalescent

corps *m:* body

à corps perdu	recklessly; without restraint
faire quelque chose à son corps défendant	to do something against one's will

côté *m:* side

à côté de la question	beside the point; off the point
côté à côté	side by side; cheek by jowl
leur voiture est grande à côté de la notre	their car is large compared to ours

coucher *v:* to go to bed, to lay down

couché à plat sur le sol	lying flat on the ground
coucher avec n'importe qui	to sleep around
coucher (ou dormir) à la belle étoile	to sleep out in the open air

coudre *v:* to sew, to sew on

il est tout cousu d'or	he is rolling in money

coup *m:* blow, cut, shot, stroke, thrust

à coup sûr	without fail; definitely
après coup	afterwards; after the event
avoir le coup de pompe	to be fagged out; to be bushed
c'est le coup de fusil; c'est de l'arnaque*	it's a rip-off; you pay through the nose
coup de foudre	unexpected event; bolt from the blue; love at first sight
donner le coup de grâce à	to give the finishing stroke to; to give the death blow
en mettre un coup	to make a big effort; to work really hard
faire coup double	to kill two birds with one stone

faire d'une pierre deux coups	*to kill two birds with one stone*
le coup de l'étrier	*one for the road*
tenir le coup	*to take it; to keep a stiff upper lip; to withstand the blow*
tout d'un coup; tout à coup	*suddenly; all of a sudden; all at once*
un coup d'épée dans l'eau	*a wasted effort*
coup *m* **d'œil:** *glance*	
il a jeté un coup d'œil vers moi	*he glanced in my direction*
couper *v:* *to cut, to chop, to cut up*	
couper la poire en deux	*to split the difference*
couper les cheveux en quatre	*to split hairs; to quibble*
couper l'herbe sous les pieds à quelqu'un	*to cut the ground from under someone*
courant *adj:* *everyday, ordinary, current, present*	
être au courant de	*to have information of; to know about; to be well-informed on*
être au courant; être au parfum	*to be in the know*
mettre quelqu'un au courant de	*to inform someone of; to put someone in the picture about*
se mettre au courant (ou au fait) de la situation	*to acquaint oneself with the situation*
tenir quelqu'un au courant de	*to keep someone informed of*
courir *v:* *to run*	
courir en tous sens	*to run in all directions*
courrier *m:* *courier, mail, post, correspondence*	
il fait son courrier	*he is dealing with his correspondence*
par le prochain courrier	*by the next post*
par retour du courrier	*by return of post*
cours *m:* *course*	
au cours de la journée	*in the course of the day; during the day*
donner libre cours à	*to give full play to; to give free rein to*

33

croire

course *f:* running, race, shopping

faire des courses	*to do some some shopping; to run errands*
arriver au pas de course	*to come running up*

coûter *v:* to cost

coûte que coûte	*at all costs; cost what it may*
coûter les yeux de la tête	*to cost an arm and a leg; to cost the earth*

coutume *f:* custom, customary

comme de coutume; comme d'habitude	*as usual*
plus (moins) que de coutume	*more (less) than usual*

couvert *m:* place setting, cover charge (restaurant)

mettre le couvert	*to lay the table; to set the table*

couvrir *v:* to cover

couvert (ou piqueté) de taches de rousseur	*freckled*

cracher *v:* to spit

il ne faut pas cracher dessus	*it's not to be sneezed at*

crever *v:* to burst, to blind

cela vous crève les yeux	*it is as clear as day; it's staring you in the face*

crier *v:* to shout, to cry out

il crie à tue-tête	*he shouts at the top of his voice; he shouts his head off*

crin *m:* horse hair

être comme un crin	*to be in a foul temper; to be cantankerous*

croc-en-jambe *m:* trip up

faire un croc-en-jambe à quelqu'un	*to trip someone up; to pull a fast one on someone*

croire *v:* to believe, to think

c'est à n'y pas croire!	*it's unbelievable!; it's beyond belief!*
il croit que c'est arrivé; il se croit sorti de la cuisse de Jupiter	*he thinks he's the cat's whiskers*
il y a tout lieu de croire que	*there is every reason to believe that*

j'ai toutes les raisons de croire que	I have every reason to believe that
je ne croyais pas si bien dire	I didn't know how right I was
je ne suis pas celle que vous croyez	I'm not that sort of person

croisière f: *cruise*

partir en croisière; faire une croisière	to go on a cruise

croix f: *cross*

croix de bois croix de fer si je mens je vais en enfer	cross my heart and hope to die
faire une croix sur quelque chose	to write something off

crucial adj: *crucial*

dans les moments cruciaux	when the chips are down

culbute f: *somersault, tumble*

faire la culbute	to fall head over heels

curieux m: *strange thing, curious thing*

le plus curieux, c'est que	the strange thing is that

D

danger m: *danger*

(il n'y a) pas de danger!	not a chance!; no fear!; don't you worry!

date f: *date*

en date de	dated; dated from; under date of

deçà adv: *this side of, short of*

deçà delà	here and there; on this side and that

décision f: *decision*

prendre une décision séance tenante	to make a decision on the spot

décoiffer v: *to disarrange the hair*

ça décoiffe	that's breathtaking; that's stunning

découvrir *v:* to discover

il a découvert le pot aux roses — *he has found out what is going on; he has got to the bottom of things*

dédaigner *v:* to despise, to scorn

ce n'est pas à dédaigner — *it is not to be sneezed (or sniffed) at*

dedans *adv:* inside

au dedans et au dehors — *inside and outside; at home and abroad*

dehors *adv:* outside, outdoors

cela ne se voit pas de dehors — *that cannot be seen from outside*

en dehors de — *outside; irrelevant to; apart from*

delà (au) *adv:* beyond

au delà il y a la rivière — *beyond that is the river*

demain *adv:* tomorrow

ce n'est pas pour demain — *it's not just round the corner; it won't happen in a hurry*

demander *v:* to ask, to ask for, to request

demander à brûle-pourpoint — *to ask point-blank*

je ne demande pas mieux — *I ask nothing better; that's just what I'd like*

je ne demande qu'à (+inf) — *all I want is to (+vb)*

demander (se) *v:* to ask oneself, to wonder

je me demande si — *I wonder whether*

démettre *v:* to dislocate

il s'est démis le bras — *he put his arm out of joint*

il s'est démis le poignet — *he dislocated his wrist*

demeurant (au) *adv:* after all

au demeurant — *after all; for all that; in fact; all things considered*

un brave homme au demeurant — *a good man, all things considered*

démission *f:* resignation

donner sa démission — *to hand in one's resignation; to resign one's post*

démoder *v:* to become outmoded

ce modèle est démodé — this model is out-of-date (or old-fashioned)

démuni,-e *adj:* unprovided

être démuni de — to be short of; to be without; to be lacking in

dent *f:* tooth

avoir les dents longues — to be ambitious; to be hungry for success

être sur les dents — to be tired; to be harassed; to be under pressure

n'avoir rien à se mettre sous la dent — not to have a bite to eat

dentelle *f:* lace

ne faire pas dans la dentelle — not to pull any punches; to go straight in

dépasser *v:* to pass, to overshoot

c'est dépassé tout ça! — that's all out of date!

dépense *f:* expense, expenditure

j'ai fait face à mes dépenses — I have met my expenses

dépenser *v:* to spend

il dépense tout son revenu — he lives up to his income

déposer *v:* to lay down, to set down

déposer quelqu'un au coin de la rue — to drop someone off at the corner

dépourvu *adj & m:* lacking, on the hop

prendre quelqu'un au dépourvu — to take (or catch) someone unawares

depuis *prep:* since, ever since, from

depuis lors; dès lors — ever since then; from that time on

depuis que; depuis le temps que — since

je travaille ici depuis longtemps — I've been working here for a long time

déranger *v:* to disturb, to disrupt

je ne vous dérange pas? — I trust that I am not disturbing you?

si cela ne vous dérange pas — if you do not mind; if that's all right by you

37

dérober *v:* to steal, to conceal
dérober un baiser à quelqu'un   to steal a kiss from someone

désaccord *m:* discord
être en désaccord avec   to be at odds (or variance) with

descendre *v:* to descend, to get out, to come down
descendre de cheval   to dismount (from a horse)
descendre de voiture (du train)   to get out of the car (the train)
descendre d'un cran   to come down off one's high horse

désemparer *v:* to quit
ils travaillent sans désemparer   they work without stopping

désespoir *m:* despair
il est au désespoir   he is in despair
en désespoir de cause   in desperation; as a last resource

désolé,-e *adj:* sorry
je suis désolé de vous avoir dérangé   I'm sorry to have disturbed you
je suis vraiment désolé   I am very (or terribly) sorry

dessous *adv & m:* under, beneath
au dessous de tout   hopeless; a disgrace; beneath contempt
avoir le dessous   to get the worst of it; to come off worst
en dessous   underneath; in an underhand manner
être dans le trente-sixième dessous   to be right down in the dumps; to be at a very low ebb

dessus *adv & m:* above, over
avoir le dessus sur   to get the better of; to have the upper hand
mettre les meilleures fraises en dessus   to put the best strawberries on top

dette *f:* debt
il a fait des dettes   he has got into debt; he has run up debts

il est criblé de dettes	he is crippled with debts; he is up to his ears in debt

deuil m: bereavement, loss

faire son deuil de quelque chose	to give something up as lost

déveine f: ill luck

avoir la déveine; être dans la déveine	to be out of luck; to have a losing streak

devoir m: duty, homework (school)

se faire un devoir de faire	to make it one's duty to do

diable m: devil

être situé au diable vauvert	to be situated miles from anywhere; to be stuck out in the countryside
fait à la diable	done any old how; scamped work
faire le diable à quatre	to create a devil of a rumpus (or shindy)
il a le diable au corps	there is no holding him; he has the devil in him
se démener comme un diable dans un bénitier	to be like a cat on hot bricks
s'en aller à tous les diables	to go to the dogs; to go to the devil
tirer le diable par le queue	to live from hand to mouth; to be hard up

différence f: difference

je n'arrive pas à trouver de différence entre eux	I cannot distinguish between them

dire v: to say, to tell

à vrai dire; à dire vrai	in actual fact; actually; to tell the truth
ça me dit	that appeals to me
ça ne me dit rien	I'm not keen on the idea; it doesn't appeal to me at all
cela va sans dire	that goes without saying
ce n'est pas pour dire, mais	just the same
c'est-à-dire	that is (to say)
c'est beaucoup dire	that's an exaggeration; that's saying a lot
c'est peu dire	that's an understatement

disposer

c'est plus facile à dire qu'à faire	it is easier said than done
comme dit l'autre	as they say
comment dirais-je ?	how shall I put it ?; what can I say ?
comment dit-on ..... en français?	how does one say ..... in French?
dire la bonne aventure à quelqu'un	to tell someone's fortune
dire que	to think that
dis donc; dites donc	tell me; I say
il a dit son façon de penser	he spoke his mind
il faut bien dire que	it must be admitted that
il n'y a pas à dire	there's no doubt about it; there's no denying it
je dois dire que tu as très bonne mine	I must say that you look very well
je vous l'avais bien dit!	I told you so!; didn't I tell you!
on a beau dire	say what you like; say what you will
on dirait de la soie	it's like silk; it feels like silk; it looks like silk
on dirait du saumon	it looks like salmon; it tastes like salmon
pour ainsi dire	so to speak; as it were
quand je vous le disais!	I told you so!; what did I tell you!
que dites-vous?; vous dites?; qu'est-ce que tu dis?	sorry!, what did you say?
sans mot dire	without saying a word
tu l'as dit!	quite true!; how right you are!

diriger v: to direct, to be in charge of

diriger ses pas vers	to make one's way towards; to make for

disparaître v: to disappear, to vanish

disparaître dans la nature	to vanish into thin air

disposer v: to arrange, dispose

être peu disposé à faire	unwilling to do; disinclined to do

disposition *f:* arrangement, disposal, (pl) aptitude
avoir des dispositions pour — to have an aptitude (or gift) for

doigt *m:* finger
croiser les doigts — to cross one's fingers
je connais les faits sur le bout du doigt — I have the facts at my fingertips
mon petit doigt me l'a dit — a little bird told me

dommage *m:* harm, damage
quel dommage!; c'est dommage! — what a pity!; what a shame!

donner *v:* to give
donner lieu à; donner sujet de — to give rise to
donner sur — to look out on to; to face; to give access to

dormir *v:* to sleep
dormir à poings fermés; dormir comme un loir; dormir comme une souche; dormir comme un sabot — to sleep like a log
dofe mouse
dormir (ou faire) la grasse matinée — to lie in bed late; to have a long lie in
dormir sur les deux oreilles — to sleep soundly

dos *m:* back
avoir sur le dos — to be saddled with; to be stuck with
en avoir plein le dos — to have had it up to here; to be fed up to the back teeth

doute *m:* doubt, uncertainty
sans doute — doubtless; no doubt; probably
sans nul doute — without any doubt
il est hors de doute que; il ne fait aucun doute que — there is no doubt that
Sans aucun doute

drap *m:* bedsheet
vous voilà dans de beaux draps — a fine mess you are in

droit *m:* right
de quel droit dites-vous cela? — what right have you to say that?

dur *m*, **dure** *f:* tough one, hard one
c'est un dur, rien ne le touche — he's very thick-skinned

41

E

écharpe *f:* scarf, sash, sling
il a le bras en écharpe — *he has his arm in a sling*
    échec *m:* failure, defeat
faire échec à quelqu'un — *to foil someone; to thwart somebody's plans*
    éclaircir *v:* to lighten, to clarify
pouvez-vous éclaircir cette question — *can you throw any light on this question?*
    éclater *v:* to explode, to burst
éclater de rire — *to burst out laughing*
    économie *f:* economics, economy, thrift
par économie — *for the sake of economy*
    écrire *v:* write, spell
comment est-ce que cela s'écrit? — *how do you spell (or write) it?*
écrire en toutes lettres — *to write out in full; to put in black and white*

    effet *m:* effect, impression
cela fait bon effet — *that gives a good impression*
    effort *m:* effort
il a fait tous ses efforts pour — *he has made every effort to*
    égal,-e *adj:* equal, even
ça m'est égal — *I don't mind; I don't care either way*
toutes choses égales — *other things being equal*
    égard *m:* consideration
à tous égards — *from every point of view; in all respects; in every respect*
par égard pour — *out of consideration for*
    embarras *m:* trouble, bother, embarrassment
se mettre dans l'embarras — *to get into difficulties; to get into a predicament*
    emblée (d') *adv:* directly, at first sight
détester quelqu'un d'emblée — *to dislike someone on sight*
    embonpoint *m:* stoutness, plumpness
il prend de l'embonpoint — *he is getting plump*

embrouiller (s') *v:* to become muddled, to become mixed up

s'embrouiller (ou s'empétrer)   to get one's knickers in a
de belle façon   twist

emporter *v:* to take, to take away

l'emporter de beaucoup sur   to be far superior to
l'emporter sur   to get the better of; to prevail
over

enceinte *adj:* pregnant

elle est enceinte de cinq mois   she is five months pregnant

enchanter *v:* to enchant, to delight

ça ne m'enchante beaucoup   that doesn't appeal to me
very much

enchanté de vous connaître   I'm very pleased to meet you;
delighted to meet you

enchère *f:* bid; **enchères** *fpl:* auction

mettre aux enchères   to put up for auction

encombre *m:* cumbrance

sans encombre   without let or hindrance;
without mishap; without a
hitch

encore *adv:* still, again

encore vous!   not you again!
quoi encore?   what is it this time?

endormir (s') *v:* to go to sleep, to fall asleep

s'endormir (ou tomber) comme   to go out like a light; to fall
une masse   asleep instantly

enfants *m, fpl:* children

les enfants en bas âge   little children; young children

entendre *v:* to hear

bien entendu   of course; understood
c'est bien entendu   that's agreed; that's
understood

j'ai entendu parler de lui   I have heard of him
j'ai entendu parler de; j'ai   I have heard (that)
entendu dire que

entendre (s') *v:* to agree, to get on

nous nous entendons très bien   we get on well together

entorse *f:* sprain, twist

faire une entorse à la vérité   to twist the truth

se donner une entorse; se faire une entorse — to sprain one's ankle

entre prep: between

entre quatre yeux — between two people; privately

sur ces entrefaites; à ce moment-là — at this juncture; at that moment

entrer v: to enter, to go in, to get in

entrer dans le vif du sujet — to get to the heart of the matter

entrer dans les vues de — to see eye to eye with

entrer en fonctions — to commence one's duties; to take office

faire entrer quelqu'un — to show someone in

je ne fais qu'entrer et sortir — I'm only stopping for a moment

envers m: inside out, wrong side, reverse

mettre à l'envers — to put on inside out; to turn inside out

envie f: envy, desire, want

j'ai envie de — I have a desire to

regarder d'un œil d'envie — to cast envious eyes upon

environ adv: about

aux environs de — about; in the neighbourhood of; in the vicinity of

envoyer v: to send

envoyer promener quelqu'un* — to send someone off with a flea in their ear

envoyer quelqu'un sur les roses* — to send someone packing

épeler v: to spell

pouvez-vous me l'épeler? — can you spell it for me?

éponge f: sponge

passons l'éponge! — let's let bygones be bygones!; let's forget all about it!; let's wipe the slate clean!

éprendre (s') v de: to be enamoured of, to fall in love with

je me suis épris d'elle — I am enamoured of her

épreuve f: test

je l'ai mis à l'épreuve — I put him (or it) to the test

to practise ones french on someone

éreinter *v:* to wear out, to pull to pieces, to slate

éreinter sous couleur d'éloge — to damn with faint praise

essai *m:* test, testing, trial

faire l'essai de — to try on; to try out

prendre quelqu'un à l'essai — to take someone on a trial basis

essayer *v:* to try, to test

j'ai beau essayer, je n'y arrive pas — however much I try, I can't do it *essayer son f... sur quelquun*

essentiel (l') *m:* the main thing

l'essentiel, c'est de (+inf) — the main (or chief) thing is to

étancher *v:* to quench, to staunch

étancher sa soif — to quench one's thirst

état *m:* state, condition

en bon état — in good condition

été *m:* summer

au cœur de l'été; au plus fort de l'été — in the height of summer

étendre *v:* to spread out, to lay out

étendu tout de son long — lying full-length; stretched out full-length

étendre (s') *v:* to stretch out, to elaborate

il s'étendit sur — he spoke at length about

étonner *v:* to amaze, to astonish, to surprise

ce qu'il y a d'étonnant, c'est que — the astonishing thing is that

étranger (l') *m:* abroad, foreign countries

il est allé à l'étranger — he has gone abroad

être *v:* to be

cela étant — that being the case

être accro — to be hooked; to have the habit

être aux aguets — to be on the look-out; to be on the watch

je n'y suis pas — I do not understand; I don't get it

où avez-vous été? — where have you been?

tu n'y es pas du tout — you do not understand at all; you haven't got it at all

45

façon

tu y es?	*are you ready?; do you follow me?*

évident,-e *adj:* obvious, evident

ce n'est pas évident	*no easy task; it's not easy to see*

excès *m:* excess, surplus

tomber d'un excès dans un autre	*to go from one extreme to another*

excuse *f:* excuse

faire des excuses; présenter ses excuses	*to apologize; to offer one's apologies*

exemple *m:* example

par exemple	*for example; for instance*

explication *f:* explanation

j'exige des explications	*I demand an explanation*

exprès *adv:* specially, on purpose

je l'ai fait exprès	*I did it on purpose*

extérieur *m:* outside, exterior, abroad

à l'intérieur et à l'extérieur	*at home and abroad; inside and outside*

F

face *f:* face

nos voisins d'en face	*our neighbours opposite*

fâché (être) *v:* to be sorry

je suis fâché de ne pas vous pouvoir aider	*I am sorry that I cannot help you*

fâcher *v:* to anger, to make angry, to vex

maintenant, tu es fâché!	*now you are angry!*
se fâcher tout rouge	*to get thoroughly angry; to blow one's top*

facile *adj:* easy

c'est facile comme tout	*it's as easy as can be*

façon *f:* way, manner

de façon inopinée	*in an unexpected (or unforeseen) manner*
d'une façon ou d'une autre	*somehow or other; in some way or another*
il fait ses façons	*he is making a fuss*

merci, sans façon — *no thanks really (or honestly)*

faillir *v:* to fail in

j'ai failli réussir — *I almost succeeded*

faillite *f:* bankruptcy

faire faillite — *to go bankrupt*

faim *f:* hunger

je crève de faim* — *I'm starving; I'm famished*

faire *v:* to do, to make

essayer en vain — *to try in vain*

faire bon/mauvais ménage — *to get on well/badly together*

faire des siennes — *to be up to one's old tricks*

il en fait à sa tête — *he does as he pleases; he goes his own way*

il fait le malade — *he is pretending to be ill*

je fais beaucoup de voiture — *I do a lot of driving*

je ne ferais cela pour rien au monde — *I wouldn't do that for anything in the world*

mettre des heures à faire quelque chose — *to take hours doing something*

n'avoir que faire de — *to have no use for*

quel métier faites-vous? — *what job do you do?; what is your line of business?*

qu'est-ce que tu fais ce soir? — *what are you doing tonight?*

sans faire ni une ni deux — *without thinking twice about it; without a moment's hesitation*

faire (s'en) *v:* to worry

t'en fais pas! — *don't let it worry you!*

faire *v* **venir:** to send for

j'ai fait venir le médecin — *I've sent for the doctor*

faire *v* **la cour:** to court, to woo

il fait la cour à Denise — *he is courting Denise*

fait *m:* event, deed, fact

au fait — *by the way; come to the point!*

en fait; de fait; par le fait — *as a matter of fact; in point of fact; in fact*

est-il au fait? — *does he know?; is he informed?*

il a été pris sur le fait — *he was caught in the act*

je lui ai dit son fait	I gave him a piece of my mind
le fait est que	the fact is that; as a matter of fact

falloir *v:* to be necessary, to be needed

il faut (+*inf*)	it is necessary to (+*vb*); we must (+*vb*)
il faut du courage pour faire ça	one needs courage to do that
il faut que je parte	I have to leave; I must leave;
que vous fallait-il faire?	what did you have to do?

faucher *v:* to reap

être fauché comme les blés	to be broke

faufiler (se) *v:* to edge (or thread) one's way

se faufilier vers la porte	to steal to the door; to edge one's way to the door

fausser *v:* to make false, to distort

il m'a faussé compagnie	he gave me the slip; he sneaked away from me

faute *f:* blame, fault, mistake, error

faire retomber la faute sur	to lay the blame on
faute de mieux	for want of something better
sans faute; à coup sûr	without fail

faux, fausse *adj:* fake, false

faire un faux pas	to stumble; to make a foolish mistake; to make a faux pas

femme *f:* woman

femme (homme) de tête	woman (man) of sense; level-headed woman (man)
une femme sage	a prudent woman

fendre (se) *v:* to crack, to fork out

se fendre de quelque chose	to fork out for something

fermer *v:* to close, to shut

je lui ai fermé la porte au nez	I closed the door in his face

feu *m:* fire, light (signal)

donner le feu vert à quelqu'un	to give someone the green light; to give the go-ahead
être tout feu tout flamme	to be very keen
il a mis le feu à la maison	he set the house on fire
il n'y a pas le feu	there's no great hurry; there's no panic

la maison a pris feu | the house has caught fire
la maison est en feu | the house is on fire
feu,-e adj: late, deceased
feu mon père; mon feu père | my late father
ficher v: to do, to put, to leave
ça me fiche la trouille | it gives me the jitters
fiche-moi le paix | leave me alone
il s'en fiche pas mal | he couldn't care less about it
je m'en fiche! | I don't care that much!; I don't give a damn!

fichu adj: done for, rotten
il est mal fichu aujourd'hui | he's off-colour today
je suis fichu | I've had it
figer v: to congeal, to clot
rester figé sur place | to remain rooted (or frozen) to the spot

figurer (se) v: to imagine
figurez-vous la situation | imagine the situation; picture the situation

filer v: to spin
filer un mauvais coton | to be in a sorry state; to get into bad ways

fils m: son
c'est bien le fils de son père | he's a chip off the old block
fin f: end
en fin de compte | at the end of the day; when all is said and done
mettre fin à | to put an end to
on n'en verra jamais la fin | we'll never see the end of this
toucher (ou tirer) à sa fin | to draw to an end
fleur f: flower
s'envoyer des fleurs | to blow one's own trumpet
foi f: faith
ma foi, c'est comme ça, mon ami | well, that's how it is my friend
foin m: hay
faire du foin | to kick up a fuss; to kick up a shindy

49

fois (une) *f:* once

une fois de plus; encore une   *once again; once more*
fois

folie *f:* madness

il a un grain de folie   *he is a little mad*

fond *m:* bottom, basis, heart, depth

à fond   *thoroughly; in depth*

au fond; dans le fond   *basically; in fact; at heart*

à fond de train   *hell for leather; full tilt; at top speed*

de fond en comble   *from top to bottom; completely*

question de fond   *fundamental question*

for *m:* forum, conscience

dans son for intérieur   *deep within one's conscience; in one's heart of hearts*

force *f:* force, strength

dans la force de l'âge   *in the prime of life*

de première force; de premier   *first-rate*
ordre

de vive force   *by main force; by sheer strength*

par la force des choses   *by force of circumstances*

forcer *v:* to force, to compel

forcer la dose   *to go too far; to overdo it*

fort,-e *adj & adv:* strong, loud, hard

c'est de plus en plus fort   *it's better and better*

c'est plus fort que moi   *I can't help it*

c'est trop fort pour moi   *it's above me; that's beyond me*

c'est un peu fort!*   *it's a bit much!; that's going a bit too far!*

et le plus fort, c'est que   *and the best part of it is that*

foudre *f:* lightning

frappé par la foudre   *struck by lightning*

la foudre tombée sur l'église   *the church was struck by lightning*

coup de foudre   *flash of lightning; unexpected event; love at first sight*

foule *f:* crowd

au plus fort de la foule/mêlée — *in the thick of the crowd/ fray*

fourmi *f:* ant

il a des fourmis dans les jambes — *he has pins and needles in his legs*

frais *mpl:* expenses, charges, costs

faire ses frais — *to cover one's expenses*

franc, franche *adj:* free, frank, open

y aller de franc jeu — *to go about it openly; to be straightforward about it*

franchir *v:* to clear, to get over

il a franchi le cap de la soixantaine — *he has turned sixty*

frayer (se) *v:* to open up, to clear

se frayer un chemin à travers la foule — *to push one's way through the crowd*

fredaine *f:* mischief, prank

faire des fredaines — *to be up to mischief; to sow one's wild oats*

frime *f:* sham, pretence

c'est de la frime — *that's a lot of eyewash; that's all window dressing*

c'est pour la frime — *it's just for show; it's just to impress*

froid *m:* cold

il fait un froid de canard — *it's bitterly cold*

froncer *v:* to gather

froncer les sourcils — *to frown; to knit one's brows*

frotter *v:* to rub

frotter une allumette — *to strike a match*

se frotter à quelqu'un — *to cross swords with someone*

fureur *f:* rage, fury

cela fait fureur — *that is all the rage*

G

gâchis m: *mess*

ils ont fait un beau gâchis de ce travail
they have made a fine mess of this job

gaffe f: *gaffe, blunder, boob*

faire une gaffe
to make a gaffe; to drop a brick; to drop a clanger

gagner v: *to earn, to gain, to win*

gagner à être connu
to improve on acquaintance

gagner à sa cause
to win over

gagner de quoi vivre
to earn one's keep

gagner du terrain
to gain ground

gagner haut la main
to win easily (or hands down)

gagner le gros lot
to hit (or win) the jackpot

gagner sa croûte; gagner son bifteck
to earn one's crust; to earn one's bread and butter

gagner sa vie; gagner son pain
to earn one's living

gagner un argent fou
to make a pile of money

gaillard m: *fellow, chap, mate*

gaillard bien bâti
strapping fellow

un vert gaillard
a sharp fellow; a sly fellow

gaillard,-e adj: *strong, well, bawdy, ribald*

contes gaillards
spicy stories

frais et gaillard
hale and hearty

galette f: *pancake, biscuit, dough (colloq)*

avez-vous de la galette?
have you got any money?

garde f: *guard, watch*

être (ou se tenir) sur ses gardes
to be on one's guard; to watch out

garder v: *to look after, to guard, to keep*

garder le lit
to stay in bed

garder le silence
to remain silent

garder son sérieux
to keep a straight face

garder une poire pour la soif
to keep something for a rainy day

garder (se) v de: *to take care not to, to be wary of*

gardez-vous de faire du bruit en entrant
take care not to make a noise when you go in

gâte-tout m, inv: *spoil-all, muddler*

il est un gâte-tout — *he's a spoilsport; he's a muddler*

gâteau m: *cake*

c'est du gâteau — *it's a piece of cake; it's a doddle*

gâter v: *to spoil, to ruin*

il pleut, on est gâté! — *it's raining, just our luck!*

geler v: *to freeze*

il gèle à pierre fendre — *it's freezing hard*

gêne f: *discomfort, financial straits*

il est dans une grande gêne — *he is in great financial difficulties*

gêner v: *to put out, to bother, to hamper*

est-ce que je vous gêne? — *am I in your way?; am I hindering you?*

il ne s'est pas gêné pour le lui dire — *he made no bones about telling him; he didn't mind telling him*

ne vous gênez pas! — *make yourself at home!; don't mind me*

si cela ne vous gêne pas — *if you don't mind; if it won't put you out*

génie m: *genius, engineering*

il est marqué au coin de génie — *he bears the stamp of genius*

genre m: *kind, type, sort*

quel genre (ou type) d'homme est-ce? — *what kind of man is he?*

gens mpl: *people*

des gens de toutes les conditions (ou de tous les milieux) — *people from all walks of life*

goût m: *taste*

à chacun son goût; chacun à son goût — *tastes differ; there is no accounting for tastes*

grâce f: *grace, favour*

faire grâce à quelqu'un de quelque chose — *to excuse; to spare someone*

grand-chose pron: *much*

ça ne vaut pas grand-chose — *it isn't worth much*

on ne sait grand-chose à ce sujet — *we don't know much about it*

personne n'y peut grand-chose — *there's not much that anyone can do about it*

grève *f: strike (industrial)*
être en grève; faire en grève — *to be on strike*
se mettre en grève — *to go on strike*

grincer *v: to grate, to grind, to gnash, to set on edge*
grincer des dents — *to grind one's teeth; to gnash one's teeth*

gros *m: bulk*
cette question est résolue en gros — *by and large (or broadly) this question is settled*

guère (ne) *adv: not much, really, hardly*
ça ne durera guère — *it won't really last*
cela ne te va guère — *that doesn't really suit you*

gueule *f: mouth (animal)*
avoir (ou faire) une gueule d'enterrement — *to look really sick; to look down in the mouth*
avoir une gueule de bois — *to have a hangover*
faire la gueule; faire la tête — *to look sulky*
tu peux crever la gueule ouverte — *you can go to hell for all I care**

guignol *m: puppet, clown*
faire le guignol — *to play the fool; to clown about; to act the clown*

guise *f de (en): by way of*
en guise de remerciement — *by way of thanks*

H

habiter *v: to live, to dwell*
j'habite dans le Yorkshire (en Grande Bretagne) — *I live in Yorkshire (in Great Britain)*
nous habitons porte à porte — *we live next door to each other*

habitude *f: habit*
comme d'habitude — *as usual*
selon mon habitude — *as I usually do*

haleine *f:* breath, breathing

reprendre haleine	*to recover one's breath; to take a breather*
tenir quelqu'un en haleine	*to hold someone spellbound; to keep someone in suspense*
tout d'une haleine	*all in one breath*

hasard *m:* chance, fate, hazard, luck

au hasard	*randomly; aimlessly; at a guess*
par hasard	*by chance; at random*
par un curieux hasard	*by a curious coincidence (or chance)*
un hasard heureux	*a stroke of luck; a stroke of good fortune*
un hasard malheureux	*a stroke of bad luck; a stroke of misfortune*

hausser *v:* to raise

hausser les épaules	*to shrug one's shoulders*

haut *m:* height, top

de haut en bas	*from top to bottom; downwards; high and low*
tout en haut d'un arbre	*right at the top of a tree*

hauteur *f:* height

être à la hauteur	*to be up to the mark; to be equal to*
il n'est pas à la hauteur	*he is not equal to it*

tenir quelqu'un en haleine

heure *f:* hour, time
à la bonne heure!   *that's fine!*
à l'heure qu'il est; à cette heure   *at this moment in time*
à pareille heure il devrait être   *at this hour (or at such a*
prêt à tout   *time) he should be ready for*
     anything

à toute heure   *at any time of the day*
de très bonne heure   *very early*
nouvelles de dernière heure   *stop-press news*
partir de meilleure heure   *to leave earlier*
passer un sale quart d'heure   *to have a nasty (or grim) time*
     of it

quelle heure avez-vous?   *what time do you make it?*
tout à l'heure   *a little while ago; just now; in*
     a little while; shortly

heurt *m:* collision, clash
sans heurts   *smoothly; without conflict*
histoire *f:* history, story
faire un tas d'histoires   *to make a great deal of fuss*
une histoire à dormir debout   *a cock-and-bull story*
homme *m:* man
l'homme moyen   *the average man; the man in*
     the street
un homme à bonnes fortunes   *a ladies' man*
honte *f:* disgrace, shame
faire honte à quelqu'un   *to put someone to shame*
horizon *m:* horizon
ils viennent d'horizons très   *they come from widely*
divers   *different backgrounds*

hors *prep:* out of, outside
cela le met hors de lui   *it drives him frantic; it*
     infuriates him

humeur *f:* mood, humour
être d'une humeur de chien   *to be in a foul temper*

I

ici *adv:* here
passez par ici!   *come this way!*

idée *f:* idea, view

avoir dans l'idée que	to have an idea that
avoir l'idée fixe	to have an obsession
il a eu l'idée lumineuse	he has had a brilliant idea (or brainwave)
il m'est venu à l'idée que	it occurred to me that

idiot,-e *adj:* silly

à question idiote, réponse idiote	ask a silly question and you'll get a silly answer

il y a: there is, there are, ago

à Londres il y a beaucoup de théâtres	in London there are many theatres
il y a belle lurette	that was ages ago; that was donkey's years ago

importer *v:* to be important, to matter

il importe peu que	it matters little that; it is not very important that
n'importe	no matter; never mind; it doesn't matter
peu importe que	it matters little whether
qu'importe?	what does it matter?

inadvertance *f:* oversight

je l'ai fait par inadvertance	I did it unintentionally; I did it by mistake

inonder *v:* to flood

inondé de lumière, inondé de clarté	flooded with light

inquiet,-ète *adj:* worried, anxious

il y a lieu d'être inquiet	there is cause (or good reason) for anxiety

instance *f:* authority, request

sur les instances pressantes de	at the earnest request of

instant *m:* moment, instant

dès l'instant où je l'ai vu	from the moment I saw him; as soon as I saw him
je n'en doute pas un seul instant	I don't doubt it for a single moment
par instants	off and on; at times

jamais

   insu *m:* without knowing
à mon insu
                without my knowledge;
                without my knowing

   intention *f:* intention
avec (ou dans) cette intention
                with this intention; for that
                (or this) purpose

   interdire *v:* to forbid, to prohibit
il est interdit de fumer
                it is forbidden to smoke;
                smoking prohibited

   interésser *v:* to interest
à quoi vous intéressez-vous?
                what are your interests?
le football ne m'intéresse pas
                I am not interested in football
   intérêt *m:* interest, benefit
il y a intérêt à (+inf)
                it is of interest to (+vb); it is
                desirable to (+vb)

   intervalle *m:* space, distance, interval
par intervalles
                at times; now and again;
                intermittently

   inventer *v:* to invent, to devise
il n'a pas inventé la poudre
                he's no bright spark; he will
                never set the Thames on fire

   irruption *f:* irruption
faire irruption dans la pièce
                to rush into the room; to
                burst into the room

   issu,-e *adj* **de:** stemming from
être issu de
                to stem from; to be
                descended from; to be born
                of

J

   jamais *adv:* ever, never (neg)
à tout jamais; pour jamais
                for ever (and ever)
je n'ai jamais de ma vie (trouvé,
                I have never in my life (found,
vu, etc)
                seen, etc)
si jamais tu passes par Paris,
                if ever you pass through
viens moi voir
                Paris, come and see me

jambe f: leg

ça lui fera une belle jambe!* — a fat lot of good that will do him!

jeter v: to throw

jeter un coup d'œil sur les enfants — to take a quick look at the children

jeu m: game, set, hand (cards)

avoir beau jeu; avoir du jeu — to have all the right cards; to have a good hand

abattre son jeu — to show one's hand; to lay one's cards on the table

joie f: joy, pleasure   *je suis   nous sommes*

être plein de joie de vivre — to be full of the joys of living

ne pas (ou ne plus) se sentir de joie — to be beside oneself with joy

jouer v: to play

il fait tout cela en se jouant — he does it all without trying

jouer à pile ou face — to spin a coin

jouer des coudes; avancer en jouant des coudes — to elbow one's way

jouer la surprise — to pretend to be surprised

ne joue pas les rabat-joie (ou les trouble-fête) — don't be such a spoilsport

jouir de v: to enjoy   *je jouis nous jouissons*

il jouit d'une bonne santé — he enjoys good health

jour m: day, daylight

au point du jour; à l'aube — at daybreak; at the crack of dawn

c'est le jour et la nuit! — there's no comparison!

il commence à faire jour — it is beginning to get light

il fait grand jour — it is broad daylight

le travail de tous les jours est intéressant — the day-to-day work is interesting

tous les deux jours — every other day; every two days

tous les jours   *parler F* — every day

voyager de jour/de nuit — to travel by day/by night

journal m: newspaper, news

à quelle heure est le journal télévisé (parlé)? — when is the television (radio) news?

nous regardons le journal télévisé

juger *v:* to judge, to decide

à en juger d'après les apparences *judging from appearances*

au jugé *by guesswork*

autant que je puisse en juger *as far as I can judge; as far as I can make out*

jusque *prep:* to, as far as, until

jusqu'à la; jusqu'au *to; as far as; right up to; all the way to*

jusqu'à quand restez-vous? *how long are you staying?*

jusqu'alors; jusques alors *up till then; until then*

jusqu'ici *until now; up to now*

jusqu'où? *how far?*

le bus vient jusqu'ici *the bus comes as far as here*

juste *adj & adv:* just, right, exact

frapper juste *to hit the nail on the head; to strike home*

rien de plus juste *you are perfectly right; nothing could be fairer*

tomber juste *to say just the right thing; to hit the nail on the head*

tout juste *only just; hardly; barely; exactly*

L

là-bas *adv:* over there, yonder

regardez là-bas *look over there*

là-dedans *adv:* inside, in there

je ne comprends rien là-dedans *I don't understand anything about it*

là-dessous *adv:* underneath, under there

il y a quelque chose là-dessous *there's more to it than meets the eye*

là-dessus *adv:* on that, thereupon, at that point

tu peux compter là-dessus *you can count on that*

là-haut *adv:* up there, upstairs, on high

il est là-haut *he is upstairs; he is in heaven*

lâcher *v:* to loosen, to let go

lâcher du lot *to make concessions*

lâcher le morceau	to let the cat out of the bag; to come clean
lâche-moi les baskets*	get off my back!; give me a break
lâcher prise	to let go; to loosen one's grip
laisser *v:* to leave, to let	
ça ne laisse pas d'être vrai	it is true nevertheless
laisser agir la nature	to let nature take its course
laissez moi faire	leave it to me
laissez-moi faire à ma guise	let me do as I like
laissez moi tranquil	leave me alone; leave me in peace; don't worry me
ne te laisse pas marcher sur les pieds	don't let anyone tread on your toes; don't let anyone take advantage of you
lancer *v:* to launch	
lancer un bateau	to launch a boat
langue *f:* tongue, language	
avoir un cheveu sur la langue	to lisp
il a la langue bien pendue; il a du bagou	he has the gift of the gab
ma langue maternelle est française	my mother tongue is French
larmes *fpl:* tears	
avoir les larmes aux yeux	to have tears in one's eyes
fondre en larmes	to burst into tears
laver *v:* to wash	
elle lave (ou fait) la vaisselle	she is washing up
lécher *v:* to lick, to lick clean	
lécher les vitrines; faire du lèche-vitrines	to go window shopping
lessive *f:* washing, wash	
elle fait la lessive	she is doing the washing
liard *m:* farthing	
ne pas avoir un rouge liard	not to have a brass farthing
lieu *m:* place	
avoir lieu	to take place
il n'y a pas lieu de (+inf)	there is no reason to
ligne *f:* line, figure	
avoir la ligne	to have a slim figure

61

lire *v:* to read

ce roman mérite d'être lu — this novel is worth reading

je l'ai lu dans le journal — I read about it in the newspaper

loin *adv:* far

du plus loin que je me souviens — as far back as I remember

j'irais même plus loin — I would go even further

je ne suis pas mécontent, bien loin de là — I'm not displeased, far from it

loin *m:* distance

au loin; dans le loin — in the distance *(notre jardin)*

lointain *m:* distance

au lointain; dans le lointain — in the distance

long *m:* length

en long et en large — in great detail; at great length

long,-ue *adj:* long

tomber tout au long — to fall at full length; to measure one's length

longtemps *adv:* (for) a long time

il habite ici depuis longtemps — he has been living here for a long time

vous en avez pour longtemps? — are you going to be long?

longue *f:* long vowel (etc), long run

à la longue — in the long run; eventually

loup *m:* wolf

il est un vieux loup de mer — he is an old sea-dog (or salt)

loustic *m:* (funny) chap, rascal

faire le loustic — to play the fool; to act the goat

lune *f:* moon

au clair de lune — in the moonlight

luné,-e *adj:* crescent-shaped, luniform

être bien/mal luné — to be in a good/bad mood

M

maille *f:* stitch, mesh

j'ai maille à partir avec toi — I have a bone to pick with you

main *f:* hand
à bas les mains! — hands off!
avoir tout sous la main — to have everything at hand
coup de main — a helping hand
donne-moi un coup de main! — give me a hand!
mettre la dernière main à — to put the finishing touch to
serrer la main de quelqu'un — to shake hands with someone

mal *adj:* bad, wrong
être mal avec quelqu'un — to be on bad terms with somebody; to be in someone's bad books

se mettre mal avec quelqu'un — to get on the wrong side of somebody; to get into someone's bad books

mal *adv:* badly, ill
être mal en point — to be in a poor way
il s'y prend mal — he goes the wrong way about it

mal *m:* evil, harm, ill
avoir mal aux cheveux — to have a hangover
il a mal au cœur — he feels sick; he has nausea
se donner un mal de chien à faire quelque chose — to go to great trouble (or bend over backwards) to do something

malade *adj:* ill, sick, unwell
tomber malade — to be taken ill

mettre la dernière main à

malchance *f:* misfortune, ill-luck

il a eu beaucoup de malchance — he's had a lot of bad luck

malheur *m:* misfortune

il va faire un malheur — he'll be a great hit; he will be a sensation

le beau malheur! — now isn't that a shame!

quel malheur! — what a pity!; how unfortunate!; what a tragedy!

manche *f:* sleeve

c'est une autre paire de manches — that's a different kettle of fish; that's another story

manche à manche — neck and neck; even; game all

manger *v:* to eat

donner à manger à quelqu'un — to give someone food (or something to eat)

manger son blé en herbe — to spend one's inheritance before one gets it

manière *f:* way, manner

de telle manière que — in such a way that

de toute manière — in any case; at any rate; anyway

d'une manière générale — generally speaking; as a general rule

en aucune manière — in no way; under no circumstances

en voilà des manières! — what a way to behave!

manquer *v:* to miss, to fail, to lack

ça ne pouvait manquer d'arriver — it was bound to happen

il me manque beaucoup — I miss him very much

le courage lui manque; il manque de courage — he lacks courage

manquer à sa parole (ou promesse) — to break one's word

manquer de (+*inf*) (ex. tomber, mourir) — to almost (+*vb*) (e.g. fall, die)

ne manquez pas de venir de bonne heure — be sure to come early

maquiller (se) v: to make up (one's face)

elle s'est maquillée avant la danse	she made up before the dance

marche f: walking

fermer la marche	to bring up the rear

marché m: market, bargain, deal

faire bon marché de; faire peu de cas de	to take little account of
faire un marché avantageux	to make (or strike) a good bargain
j'ai acheté tous mes livres à bon marché	I bought all my books cheaply
marché conclu!	it's a deal!
par-dessus le marché	into the bargain; on top of all that

marcher v: to march, to tread, to work

ça marche comme sur des roulettes	it is all going smoothly; it is going like clockwork
faire marcher quelqu'un	to get a rise out of someone; to pull someone's leg
marcher à pas de loup	to walk stealthily; to creep along
marcher à quatre pattes	to go on all fours; on one's hands and knees
marcher à reculons	to walk backwards
marcher sur des œufs	to skate on thin ice; to tread on delicate ground
tout marche à souhait	everything is going splendidly

mariage m: marriage

faire un mariage d'inclination (ou d'amour)	to marry for love
il a fait un riche mariage	he has married into money
il lui a fait une demande en mariage	he proposed to her

marmotter v: to mumble

arrête de marmotter; arrête de parler entre tes dents	stop mumbling

marquer *v:* to mark, to stamp
il est marqué au bon coin — *he is a man of the right stamp; he is a man of commonsense*

matin *m:* morning
de bon matin; de grand matin — *very early in the morning*

mauvais,-e *adj:* bad
se faire du mauvais sang — *to fret; to worry; to get into a state*

méchant *adj:* spiteful, nasty, wicked, naughty
devenir méchant — *to turn nasty (or spiteful)*

mèche *f:* wick, fuse
vendre la mèche; éventer la mèche — *to let the cat out of the bag; to give the game away*

mégarde (par) *adv:* inadvertently
par mégarde — *inadvertently; accidentally; by mistake*

mêler (se) *v:* to mix, to involve oneself, to meddle with
mêlez-vous de ce qui vous regarde! — *mind your own business!*

même *adj & adv:* same, even
c'est du pareil au même — *it comes to the same thing; it makes no odds*
c'est la même chose — *it's all the same; it makes no odds*

vendre la mèche

cela revient au même	it amounts to the same thing
elle fera de même	she'll do the same; she'll do likewise
être à même de (+inf)	to be in a position to (+vb); to be able to (+vb)
oh, quand même?	oh, really?
tout de même; quand même	all the same; nevertheless

mémoire f: memory

si j'ai bonne mémoire	if I remember rightly

ménage m: housekeeping, housework

faire bon ménage	to get on well together
faire le ménage	to do the housework
tenir le ménage	to look after one's house; to keep house

mener v: to lead, to take

mener à la baguette	to boss around; to have under one's thumb

méninges fpl: brain

se triturer (ou se creuser) les méninges	to rack one's brains

mentir v: to lie

il ment comme il respire	he is a born liar

méprendre (se) v: to make a mistake, to be mistaken

il n'y a pas à s'y méprendre	there is no mistaking it

mépris m: contempt, scorn, disregard

il n'a pas le mépris des convenances	he has no regard for the conventions

mer f: sea

mettre à la mer; prendre la mer	to put to sea; to launch a boat

merveille f: marvel, wonder

faire des merveilles; faire des prodiges	to work wonders

mesure f: extent, measure, measurement

à mesure que; au fur et à mesure que	as; (proportionally) as; as soon as
dans la mesure de mes forces (ou capacités)	as far as I am able; to the best of my ability
dans la mesure du possible	as far as possible

mettre

dans une certaine mesure	*to a certain extent; to some extent*

mesurer *v:* *to measure, to match, to assess*

mesurer sa dépense à ses revenus	*to live within one's means*

météo *f abb:* *weather forecast*

la météo est bonne aujourd'hui	*the weather forecast is good today*

mettre *v:* *to put, to put on*

il est bien mis	*he is well dressed*
mettons que	*let's suppose that*
mettons que j'aie raison	*let's suppose that I am right*
mettre à jour	*to bring up to date*
mettre au jour	*to bring to light; to reveal*
mettre dans le mille; mettre dans le noir	*to hit the bull's-eye; to hit the nail on the head*
mettre du foin dans ses bottes	*to feather one's nest*
mettre le cap sur le port	*to head for port (ship)*
mettre le doigt dessus	*to put one's finger on it; to hit the nail on the head*
mettre quelque chose en train	*to get something going (or under way)*
mettre quelqu'un dedans	*to take someone in; to get someone confused*
mettre son grain de sel	*to put one's oar in*
mettre un peu d'argent de côté	*to put (or set) a little money aside*
mettre un projet à exécution	*to carry out a plan*

Vous avez mis le doigt dessus

mettre le doigt dessus

se mettre à prendre des
somnifères   *to start taking sleeping pills*

mettre (se) *v:* to put, to put oneself
se mettre en colère   *to get angry*
se mettre en quatre pour *(+inf)* *to strain every nerve to; to do*
                                  anything for
se mettre martel en tête   *to get worried; to get worked*
                                  up

midi *m:* midday, noon, lunchtime
vers midi   *about midday; about lunch-*
                                  time

mieux *adj & adv:* better
d'autant mieux   *all the better; even better*
il se porte mieux; il va mieux   *he is better*
je le sais mieux que quiconque   *I know that better than*
                                  anybody
tant mieux   *so much the better; that's*
                                  fine

mieux *m:* best
faire quelque chose de son   *to do something to the best*
mieux   *of one's ability*

mine *f:* expression, look
avoir la mine longue (ou allongée) *to have (or to pull) a long*
                                  face
quelle mine a-t-elle? elle a   *how does she look? she*
bonne mine   *looks well*
tu n'as pas bonne mine   *you do not look well*

minuit *m:* midnight
sur le coup de minuit   *on the stroke of midnight*

mise *f:* attire, clothing
soigner sa mise   *to be particular in one's*
                                  dress; to take pride in one's
                                  appearance

mise *f:* putting, stake
être de mise   *to be in circulation; to be*
                                  fashionable

mode *f:* fashion
passé de mode   *out of date; out of fashion*

mœurs *fpl:* customs, habits, morals

autres temps, autres mœurs	customs (or manners) change with the times
entrer dans les mœurs	to become a way of life; to become normal practice
une affaire (ou histoire) de mœurs	a sex scandal; a sex case

moins *adv & prep:* less, least

elle n'était pas le moins du monde fatigué	she was not in the least tired
en moins de rien	in less than no time
il était moins une (ou cinq)!*	it was a close shave!; it was a near thing!

moitié *f:* half

on a partagé le gateau moitié moitié	we halved the cake between us; we shared the cake half and half
se mettre de moitié avec quelqu'un	to go halves with someone

moment *m:* moment

à (ou dans) ses moments perdus	in his or her spare time
à tout moment	at any moment
au bon moment	in the nick of time; just at the right time
du moment que	seeing that; as long as; since
en ce moment	at the moment; at this time; at present
j'attends son arrivée d'un moment à l'autre	I expect him to arrive any moment now
par moments	at times; from time to time; now and then
pour le moment	for the time being; at present
sur le moment	for a moment; at the time

monde *m:* world

il faut de tout pour faire un monde	it takes all sorts to make a world
il y a un monde entre les deux	there's a world of difference between the two; they are worlds apart

je ne ferais cela pour rien au monde — *I wouldn't do that for anything in the world*

monnaie f: *change, currency*

je n'ai pas de monnaie — *I have no change*

petite monnaie — *small change*

montagne f: *mountain*

se faire une montagne de rien — *to make a mountain out of a molehill*

moquer (se) v: *to make fun of, to laugh at*

je m'en moque comme de l'an quarante — *I don't care two pins about it*

moral m: *morale*

avoir le moral — *to be feeling great*

avoir le moral à zéro — *to be down in the dumps*

mors m: *bit*

il a pris le mors aux dents — *he took the bit between his teeth*

mort f: *death*

être à deux doigts de la mort — *to be within an ace of death; to be at death's door*

être à l'article de la mort — *to be at death's door*

mort,-e adj: *dead*

plus mort que vif — *more dead than alive; scared stiff*

mot m: *word*

dans toute l'acception du mot — *in every sense of the word*

faire des mots — *to make witty remarks*

prendre quelqu'un au mot — *to take somone at his or her word*

mouche f: *fly*

faire la mouche du coche — *to be as busy as a bee; to be fussing around; to be a busybody*

prendre la mouche — *to flare up; to get huffy; to go off in the sulks*

quelle mouche t'a piqué? — *what has bitten you?*

mouchoir m: *handkerchief*

finir dans un mouchoir — *to be a close finish*

mouiller v: *to wet, to drench*

mouillé jusqu'aux os — *drenched to the skin*

mouiller *v:* to implicate, to compromise
il ne veut pas se mouiller   *he does not want to get*
                                     involved

mourir *v:* to die
je meurs d'envie de le revoir!   *I can't wait to see him again!*
mourir de chagrin   *to die of grief; to die of a*
                                     broken heart
mourir de faim   *to starve to death; to die of*
                                     hunger
mourir de sa belle mort   *to die a natural death*
mourir d'ennui   *to be bored to tears*

mouvement *m:* movement, motion
suivre le mouvement; prendre   *to jump on the bandwagon*
le train en marche

moyen *m:* means, way; **moyens** *mpl:* means
de tous les moyens dont il   *with every means at his*
dispose   *disposal*
il n'y a pas moyen de moyenner   *there's no way it can be done*
je n'en ai pas les moyens   *I cannot afford it*
par tous les moyens   *by fair means or foul; by*
                                     hook or by crook; by every
                                     way possible
trouver moyen de (+inf)   *to find a way to*

moyenne *f:* average
en moyenne   *on (an) average*

N

nage *f:* swimming, swim stroke, sweat
faire un 100 m nage libre   *to swim 100 m freestyle*
je suis en nage (ou en sueur)   *I am perspiring*
nage sous-marine   *under-water swimming*
se mettre en nage   *to begin to perspire; to get*
                                     into a lather

naître *v:* to be born
être né coiffé   *to be born with a silver spoon*
                                     in one's mouth; to be born
                                     lucky
être né sous une bonne étoile   *to be born under a lucky star*

nécessaire *adj:* necessary

il est nécessaire de le faire — it needs to be done; it's necessary to do it

neuf *m:* new

faire du neuf — to introduce new ideas

quoi de neuf chez vous? — what's your news?

nez *m:* nose

avoir un verre dans le nez — to have had one too many; to be tipsy

faire un pied de nez — to thumb one's nose; to cock a snook

il parle du nez — he talks through his nose

niche *f:* niche, kennel, trick, hoax

faire des niches à quelqu'un — to play tricks on someone

nième, énième *adj:* nth, umpteenth

pour la nième fois — for the umpteenth time

Noël *m:* Christmas

joyeux Noël — happy Christmas; merry Christmas

nostalgie *f:* nostalgia, homesickness

avoir la nostalgie de son pays — to feel homesick

notoriété *f:* notoriety, fame

c'est de notoriété publique — that's common knowledge

nouveau (de) *adv:* again

faire quelque chose de nouveau — to do something again; to repeat something

nouvelle(s) *f, fpl:* news

vous connaissez la nouvelle? — have you heard the news?

je voudrais bien avoir de ses nouvelles — I should like to have news of him

nuit *f:* night, darkness

à la faveur de la nuit — under cover of darkness

dans la nuit des temps — in the deep, dark past; in the mists of time

fort avant dans la nuit — far into the night; in the small hours of the morning

il se fait nuit — it is getting (or growing) dark

j'ai passé une nuit blanche (ou nuit sans sommeil) — I had a sleepless night

nul, nulle *adj:* no, nil, useless

ils ont fini par faire match nul (ou partie nulle)	the match ended in a draw
nul autre que moi ne le sait	no one else except me knows of it

O

obvier *v:* to overcome

obvier (ou parer) à un inconvénient	to overcome a difficulty (or snag)

occasion *f:* occasion, opportunity, bargain

à la première occasion	at the first opportunity; at your earliest convenience
quelle occasion!	what a bargain!

occuper *v:* to occupy

je suis très occupé en ce moment	I am very busy at present

œil *m:* eye (see also yeux)

avoir le compas dans l'œil	to have a good eye; to have good judgement
en un clin d'œil	in a trice; in the twinkling of an eye
il a l'œil au guet	he is keeping a sharp look out
se mettre le doigt dans l'œil	to be mistaken; to be on the wrong track; to be kidding oneself

œillade *f:* glance, wink

lancer des œillades à quelqu'un	to make eyes at someone

œuf *m:* egg

plein comme un œuf	chock-full; full to bursting

œuvre *f:* work

se mettre à l'œuvre	to set to work; to get down to work

ombre *f:* shade, shadow, obscurity

elle ne le quitte pas plus que son ombre	she sticks to him as close as his shadow
n'être plus que l'ombre de soi-même	to be only a shadow of one's former self

se tenir (ou rester) dans l'ombre   *to keep in the background*

    or *m:*   gold

c'est de l'or en barre   *it's a rock-solid investment;*
it's a gold mine

    ordinaire *adj & m:*   ordinary, normal

comme d'ordinaire; comme à   *as usual; usually*
l'ordinaire

    ordre *m:*   order

mettre de l'ordre (ou en ordre)   *to tidy up the room*
dans la chambre

    ordres *mpl:*   orders, Holy Orders

entrer dans les ordres   *to be ordained; to enter the*
Church

recevoir les ordres   *to be ordained; to take Holy*
Orders

    oreille *f:*   ear

avoir l'oreille basse   *to look crestfallen; to have*
one's tail between one's legs

il a l'oreille dure   *he is hard of hearing*

    os *m:*   bone, snag

il ne fera pas de vieux os   *he won't live long; he won't*
live to an old age

il y a un os   *there's a snag; there's a hitch*

trouver (ou tomber sur) un os   *to find (or hit) a snag*

    où *pron:*   where

où diable a-t-il mis ses   *where the dickens has he*
chaussures!   *put his shoes!*

P

    pain *m:*   bread

avoir du pain sur la planche   *to have a lot to do*

    papier *m:*   paper

être dans les petits papiers de   *to be in the good books of*

    parages *mpl:*   region

dans ces parages   *in this region; in these parts*

    parcourir *v:*   to go over, to traverse

parcourir au pas de course   *to run along (a path, road)*

pareil,-eille *adj:* the same, similar, alike

il n'y en pas deux pareils — *there are no two alike (or the same)*

parent *m:* parent, relative

ils sont proches parents — *they are closely related; they are close relatives*

parfois *adv:* sometimes, at times, occasionally

il arrive parfois que — *it happens sometimes that*

parfum *m:* perfume, scent, fragrance

quel parfum délicat! — *what a delicate scent (or fragrance)!*

parler *v:* to speak, to talk

elle me parle à l'oreille (ou à voix basse) — *she whispers to me*

n'en parlez pas — *don't mention it; don't speak about it*

parler à cœur ouvert — *to speak freely; to unbosom oneself*

parler à tort et à travers — *to speak at random; to blather*

parler avec abondance — *to speak fluently*

parler chiffons — *to talk fashions; to talk clothes*

parler d'abondance — *to speak off the cuff; to extemporize; to speak at length*

parler d'affaires — *to talk business; to talk shop*

parler haut; parler à haute voix — *to speak up*

parler sans ambages — *to speak frankly*

parler sans détours — *to speak frankly; to speak plainly*

sans parler de — *not to mention; to say nothing of; let alone*

se parler à cœur ouvert — *to speak freely to one another; to have a heart-to-heart talk*

vous n'avez qu'à parler — *just say the word; you've only to say the word*

parole *f:* word, speech

elle a la parole facile — *she has a ready tongue; she is a fluent speaker*

paroles aigres — *sharp words; cutting words*

prendre la parole pour dire — *to take the floor to speak; to commence to speak*

tenir parole — *to keep one's word; to be as good as one's word*

voilà une bonne parole! — *sound thinking!*

part *f:* share, part, on one side

faire bande à part — *to go it alone; to keep to oneself; to form a separate group*

partager *v:* to divide, to share

je ne partage pas cette opinion — *I do not share that view*

parti *m* **pris:** prejudice, bias

avoir un parti pris pour quelqu'un — *to have a bias towards someone*

être de parti pris — *to be biased*

juger sans parti pris — *to take an unbiased view*

parti,-e *adj:* part

être complètement parti — *to be plastered (intoxicated)*

être un peu parti (ou legèrement ivre) — *to be tipsy*

partie *f:* part, party (person)

faire partie intégrant de — *to be an integral part of; to be part and parcel of*

une partie carrée — *a foursome (two men, two women); a wife-swapping party*

partir *v:* to go, to leave, to depart

à partir de cet instant — *from that moment*

partir comme un éclair — *to go off like a flash (or greased lightning)*

partir comme un trait — *to go off like a shot*

partir en tapinois — *to slip away*

partout *adv:* everywhere

partout où — *everywhere that; wherever*

77

passe *f:* pass

vous êtes en bonne passe — you are in a strong position; it's all plain sailing

passer *v:* to pass, to go, to proceed

en passant — in passing; by the way

il faut que ça passe ou ça casse — it's make or break

passer à l'ordre du jour — to proceed to the business of the day

passer aux choses sérieuses — to get down to business

passer dans la rue — to go down the street

passer-moi l'expression — if you'll excuse the expression

passer un examen; se présenter à un examen — to sit for an examination

passer (se) *v:* to take place, to happen

que se passe-t-il? — what's the matter?; what's happening?; what's going on?

patience *f:* patience

prendre (ou s'armer de) patience — to have patience; to be patient

pause *f:* break

faire une pause café — to have a coffee break

payer *v:* to pay, to settle

il faut payer d'effronterie — we must brazen it out

il me le paiera cher! — I'll make him pay for that!

s'en payer une tranche — to have a great time; to have a high old time; to have a lot of fun

peau *f:* skin

avoir quelqu'un dans la peau — to have got someone under one's skin; to be crazy about someone

il a fait peau neuve — he has turned over a new leaf

pêche *f:* peach, slap

avoir la pêche — to be in fine fettle; to be in top form

donner une pêche à quelqu'un — to slap someone across the face

peine *f:* penalty, sorrow, effort

avec/sans peine	with/without difficulty
ce n'est pas la peine de (+inf)	it is not worth while; there is no point in
porter la peine de	to pay the penalty for; to suffer for; to be punished for

pelote *f:* ball

faire sa pelote	to feather one's nest; to make one's pile

pendant *prep:* during

pendant ce temps	during this time; meanwhile

pendant que *conj:* while, whilst

pendant qu'il se réposait, elle faisait le ménage	while he rested, she did the housework

pendre *v:* to hang, to put up

ça nous pend au nez!	there's trouble coming our way!

penser *v:* to think

ne penser qu'à ça	to have a one-track mind; to have sex on the mind
pensez donc!	just imagine!; just think!
pensez si j'étais furieux!	you can imagine how angry I was!

pension *f:* pension, allowance

pension alimentaire	living allowance; alimony (or maintenance) allowance

perdre *v:* to lose

je suis perdu!	I'm done for!; it's all up with me!
j'y perds mon latin	I can't make head nor tail of it
perdre le fil	to lose one's train of thought
perdre l'équilibre	to lose one's balance
perdre (ou céder) du terrain	to lose ground

perte *f:* loss

en pure perte	to no purpose; fruitlessly; for absolutely nothing

petit,-e *adj:* small, little

petit à petit; peu à peu	little by little; gradually

pétrin *m:* mess, jam, fix

être dans le pétrin	to be in the soup; to be in a jam

peu *adv:* little, not much

peu après/avant	shortly after/before

peur *f:* fear

il a eu plus de peur que de mal	he was more frightened than hurt
n'ayez pas peur	do not be afraid

peut-être *adv:* perhaps, maybe

peut-être bien	it may well be; maybe so, maybe not

pied *m:* foot

avoir les pieds plats	to be flat-footed
de pied en cap	from head to foot; from top to toe
faire quelque chose au pied levé	to do something straight off; to do something at a moment's notice
lâcher pied	to give way; to give ground; to retreat
mettre les pieds dans le plat	to put one's foot in it
mettre quelqu'un au pied du mur	to corner someone; to drive someone into a corner
perdre pied	to be out of one's depth; to lose one's footing
sauter (ou aller) à cloche-pied	to hop (on one foot)
se lever du pied gauche	to get out of bed on the wrong side
sur le même pied; sur un pied d'égalité	on an equal footing; as equals

piger *v:* to twig, to understand

il a pigé	he's twigged; the penny has dropped; he's cottoned on

pile *adv:* sharp (time), dead (stop)

il est dix (etc) heures pile	it's ten (etc) o'clock sharp (or on the dot)

pile *f:* battery, pile, stack

à pile ou face?	heads or tails?

c'est à pile ou face	*it's a toss-up; it's heads or tails*

pince *f:* crowbar, leg
aller à pinces*	*to foot it; to hoof it; to go on foot*

pique-assiette *m, f, inv:* scrounger, sponger
il est un pique-assiette	*he is a sponger (or parasite)*

piquer *v:* to inject, to prick, to sting
piquer une tête dans la piscine	*to dive headfirst into the pool*
piquer quelqu'un au vif	*to sting someone to the quick*
piquer une crise	*to hit the roof; to have a fit*

pire *m:* worse
ça donne lieu de craindre le pire	*that leads one to fear the worse*
on n'a pas vu le pire	*there's worse to come*

pis *adj & adv:* worse, worst
aller de pis en pis	*to get worse and worse*
au pis aller	*at the worst; if the worst comes to the worst*

pis-aller *m, inv:* last resort
ce serait un pis-aller	*that would be a last resort (or stopgap)*

pistonner *v:* to pull strings for
se faire pistonner	*to get someone to pull strings; to get strings pulled*

pitié *f:* pity
prendre quelqu'un en pitié	*to take pity on someone*

place *f:* place, position, room (space)
de place en place; par places	*here and there; in places*
il n'y a pas de place	*there is no room; there isn't a vacancy*
mettez-vous à ma place	*put yourself in my position*
on n'a pas de place pour se retourner	*there's no room to move*
prendre de la place	*to take up a lot of room (or space)*
prendre place	*to take one's seat*
si j'étais à votre place	*if I were you; if I were in your place*

pleuvoir   *je ne peut pas !*

placer *v:* to place, to put, to invest
ne pas pouvoir placer un mot   not to be able to get a word
courtyans   in edgeways
placer de l'argent   to invest money; to deposit
                                                             money

plaire *v:* to enjoy, to please, to like
elle se plaît à Venise   she enjoys being in Venice
je travaille quand ça me plaît   I work when I feel like it
le concert vous a-t-il plu?   did you enjoy the concert?
plaire à quelqu'un   to please someone; to be
                                                             agreeable to someone

plaisanterie *f:* jest, joke
faire une plaisanterie   to tell (or crack) a joke
il a pris notre plaisanterie du bon   he took our joke in good part
côté
il l'a dit par plaisanterie   he said it in jest   *je l'ais dit*
                                                                                    par p. !
plaisir *m:* pleasure, delight
faire plaisir à quelqu'un   to please someone
je trouve beaucoup de plaisir à la   I really enjoy music
musique

planche *f:* board, plank
faire la planche   to float on one's back

planter *v:* to plant, to put in, to stick
elle m'a planté là   she jilted me; she walked out
                                                             on me
planter là   to dump; to ditch; to pack in;
                                                             to leave in the lurch

plaque *f:* sheet, slab, block
mettre à côté de la plaque   to be off track; to have
                                                             missed the point

plat,-e *adj:* flat, level
faire du plat à quelqu'un   to chat someone up; to toady
                                                             up to someone

pleurer *v:* to cry, to weep
être sur le point de pleurer   to be on the verge of tears
pleurer comme un veau (ou une   to cry one's eyes out
madeleine)
pleuvoir *v:* to rain
les jours où il pleut   on rainy days; on days when
                                                             it rains

82

plier v.: to fold, to bend

plier bagage	to pack up and go; to get out; to clear off
se mettre (ou se plier) en quatre pour aider quelqu'un	to lean over backwards to help someone

plume f.: feather, pen

y laisser des plumes	to suffer a loss; to get one's fingers burnt

plus adv.: more

pronounce s ?

de plus; en outre	furthermore
de plus en plus	more and more

plutôt adv.: rather

elle est plutôt intelligente	she's rather a clever person

poil m.: hair

à poil	starkers; in one's birthday suit; naked
au poil; au quart de poil	great; fantastic; smashing; perfection
avoir un poil dans la main	to have a lazy streak; to be work-shy
de tout poil	of all kinds; of every shape and size
être de bon/mauvais poil*	to be in a good/bad mood
se mettre à poil	to strip off

point m.: point, dot, position

jusqu'à un certain point	to some degree; up to a point; to a certain extent
mettre au point	to perfect; to finalize; to settle

poisson m.: fish

donner un poisson d'avril à	to make an April fool of

pompe f.: pump, press-up

faire des pompes; faire des tractions	to do press-ups (or push-ups)

porte f.: door

mettre quelqu'un à la porte	to sack someone; to turn someone out of the house

porter v.: to carry, to bring, to wear

cela porte bonheur; cela porte chance	it brings good luck; it brings good fortune

83

pouffer

cela porte malheur	*it brings bad luck; it brings misfortune*
je porte mon porte-bonheur partout où je vais	*I carry my lucky charm everywhere I go*
porter de l'eau à la rivière (ou à la mer)	*to carry coals to Newcastle*
porter en bandoulière	*to carry over the shoulder*
porter le chapeau	*to carry the can*
porter le dernier coup (ou le coup fatal) à nos projets	*to prove fatal to our plans*

porter (se) *v:* to be (well, etc)

je me porte à merveille	*I am wonderfully well; I am in excellent health*

portion *f:* portion, share

être réduit à la portion congrue	*to be down to the bare essentials; to get the smallest share*

poser *v:* to put down, to set down, to stand up

poser un lapin à quelqu'un*	*to stand someone up*

possible *adj:* possible

c'est pas possible!	*you don't say!; well I never!; that's impossible!*
je ferai tout mon possible	*I will do my utmost*
si possible je voudrais aller à l'opéra	*if possible I should like to visit the opera*

poste *f:* post, mail

envoyé (ou expédié ou mise) à la poste	*sent by post; posted*

pouce *m:* thumb

coup de pouce	*push in the right direction; finishing touches; final touch*
et le pouce!	*and a bit more (besides)!*
lever le (ou faire du) pouce	*to thumb a lift*
manger sur le pouce	*to have a snack*
mettre les pouces	*to knuckle under; to give in; to give up*
se tourner les pouces	*to twiddle one's thumbs*
voyager sur le pouce	*to thumb a lift; to hitch-hike*

pouffer *v de rire:* to laugh, to giggle

avoir le fou rire	*to giggle*

il se pouffait de rire — he was bubbling over with laughter

poule *f:* hen
c'est une poule mouillée — he cannot say boo to a goose
quand les poules auront des dents — when pigs can fly

pourquoi *adv & conj:* why
pourquoi faire? — what(ever) for?
pourquoi pas? — why not?

poursuivre *v:* to pursue, to sue, to prosecute
poursuivre quelqu'un en dommages-intérêts — to sue someone for damages

pourvu que *conj:* provided that, let's hope
pourvu qu'il vienne — let's hope he comes; provided that he comes; so long as he comes

pousser *v:* to push, to drive, to grow
il a me poussé à bout — he exhausted my patience; he drove me to the limit
pousser dans ses derniers retranchements — to drive into a corner

pouvoir *v:* to be able
il se peut que — it is possible that
on n'y peut rien — there's nothing one can do about it; it cannot be helped

préférence *f:* preference
de préférence à — in preference to; rather than

préférer *v:* to prefer
il préfère que ce soit vous qui le fassiez — he would rather you did it
je préfère lire un roman de science-fiction — I prefer reading a science-fiction novel
je préférerais que vous veniez vous-même — I would rather you came yourself

prendre *v:* to take, to catch
à tout prendre — on the whole; all in all
c'est à prendre ou à laisser — take it or leave it
il faut en prendre et en laisser — you can only believe half of what he says

prétexte

il y a à prendre et à laisser	it's like the curate's egg — good in parts
je vous ai pris pour quelqu'un d'autre	I took you for someone else
prendre en grippe	to take a sudden dislike to
prendre goût à	to acquire a taste (or liking) for
prendre (ou monter dans) le train en marche	to jump on to the bandwagon
prendre quelqu'un la main dans le sac	to catch someone red-handed
prendre son essor	to take flight (bird); to spring into life; to develop rapidly
prendre un bol d'air	to go out for a breather; to take a breather
prendre une maison à bail	to take a house on lease
s'en prendre à	to pick on; to take it out on; to lay blame on
si je les y prends!	let me catch them at it!

près *adv:* near, close

de près	near to; closely

présence *f:* presence

faire acte de présence	to put in a token appearance

présenter *v:* to introduce, to present

je vous présent ma femme	have you met my wife?; may I introduce my wife

presser *v:* to press, to squeeze, to hurry

je suis pressé	I'm in a hurry
presser le pas (ou l'allure)	to hurry on; to quicken one's pace

prêt,-e *adj:* ready

tout est prêt	everything is ready

prêter *v:* to lend

pourriez-vous me prêter votre parapluie?	could you lend me your umbrella?

prétexte *m:* pretext, excuse

sous aucun prétexte; en aucun cas	under no circumstances; on no account

prière *f:* prayer

fais une petite prière pour moi — *keep your fingers crossed for me*

privé,-e *adj:* private

est-ce que je peux vous parler en privé? — *can I speak to you in private?*

prix *m:* price, cost

au plus juste prix — *at the lowest price; at rock-bottom price*

aux prix où est le beurre — *prices being what they are*

prix courant; tarif — *price-list*

probabilité *f:* probability, likelihood

selon toutes probabilités; selon toute vraisemblance — *in all probability; in all likelihood*

procès *m:* proceedings (legal)

intenter un procès à — *to bring an action against; to start proceedings against*

procès-verbal *m:* report, statement

procès-verbal — *official report; statement; minutes*

prodige *m:* marvel, wonder

faire des prodiges — *to work wonders*

profit *m:* profit, benefit, advantage

mettre à profit — *to turn to good account; to take advantage of*

progrès *m:* progress

vous êtes en progrès; vous faites des progrès — *you are improving; you are making progress*

proie *f:* prey

devenir la proie de — *to fall prey to; to become prey to*

promenade *f:* walk, stroll

faire une promenade — *to go for a walk (or stroll)*

promener (se) *v:* to walk

se promener de long en large — *to walk up and down*

promesse *f:* promise

tenir sa promesse — *to keep one's promise*

propos (à) *m:* purpose, aptness, timely, opportune

à ce propos — *with reference to this; in this connection*

à propos, dis-moi	*by the way, tell me*
arriver fort à propos; arriver juste à temps	*to arrive in the nick of time*
cela manque d'à propos	*that is not to the point*
c'est à quel propos?	*what is it about?; what is it in connection with*

propre *adj:* own, specific, clean

les coutumes propre à certaines regions	*the customs peculiar to (or characteristic of) certain regions*
réussir par ses propres moyens	*to succeed by one's own efforts*

protester *v:* to protest

j'ai protesté comme un beau diable	*I protested for all I was worth*

prudence *f:* care, caution, prudence

agir avec prudence	*to use discretion*

puce *f:* flea, microchip

avoir la puce à l'oreille	*to be uneasy; to be suspicious*
mettre la puce à l'oreille à quelqu'un	*to put a flea in someone's ear; to arouse someone's suspicions*

Q

qualité *f:* quality, position, capacity

avoir qualité pour	*to have authority to*
en sa qualité de directeur	*in his capacity (or position) as manager*
la cuisine est de première qualité ici	*the food is first-rate here; the food is top quality here*

quand *conj:* when

quand bien même	*even though; even if*

quantième *m:* day of the month

à quel quantième sommes-nous?	*what day of the month is it?; what date is it?*

quatre *adj & m:* four

se mettre en quatre pour
quelqu'un

to go to great trouble to
help someone

que *pron:* what

que dire?

what could I say?

que faire?

what's to be done?

quel, quelle *adj & pron:* what, which, whoever, whatever

quel que soit le résultat, je le
ferai

whatever the result, I will do
it

quelque *adj:* some

mettez votre valise quelque
part dans le coin

put your bag somewhere in
the corner

quelque chose *pron:* something

ça alors, c'est quelque chose!

that's a bit much!

faire quelque chose à quelqu'un

to have an effect on someone

querelle *f:* quarrel

chercher querelle à quelqu'un

to pick a quarrel with
someone

question *f:* question, query

je voudrais poser une question

I would like to ask a question

la question n'est pas là

that's not the point

pas question!

out of the question!; not on
your life!

queue *f:* queue

faire la queue

to line up in a queue

quiconque *pron:* anyone, anybody, whoever

je le sais mieux que quiconque

I know that better than
anyone

quinze *adj:* fifteen

pour quinze jours; pour une
quinzaine

for a fortnight

quitter *v:* to leave, to quit

en être quitte à bon compte

to get off lightly; to be well
out of it

quoi *pron:* what

à quoi bon? (faire quelque chose)

what is the use? (of doing
something)

il n'y a pas de quoi

don't mention it; not at all;
you're welcome

quoi que nous fassions

whatever we do

raison

quoi qu'il arrive	*whatever happens; come what may*
quoi qu'il en soit	*however that may be; be that as it may*

quotidien m: *daily (news)paper*

je suis abonné à un quotidien	*I take a daily paper*

R

raccourci m: *short cut*

prendre un raccourci	*to take a short cut*

raconter v: *to tell, to relate*

il raconte n'importe quoi	*he's talking rubbish (or nonsense)*
raconter une histoire	*to tell a story; to spin a yarn*

radio f: *radio*

à la radio	*on the radio*
c'est le signal horaire à la radio	*it's the time signal on the radio*
mets la radio	*turn (or put) on the radio*

radis m: *radish*

n'avoir plus un radis (ou le sou)	*not to have a bean left*

raffoler v: *to be very keen on*

je raffole de la musique	*I am passionately fond of music*

raie f: *line, furrow, parting*

se faire une raie	*to part one's hair*

raison f: *reason, right*

avoir raison de quelqu'un; triompher de quelqu'un	*to get the better of someone*
donner raison à quelqu'un	*to admit someone is right*
en raison de	*on account of; due to; because of*
la raison pour laquelle	*the reason why*
mettre quelqu'un à la raison	*to bring someone to his senses; to talk some sense into someone*
pour une raison quelconque	*for some reason or other*
tu as raison	*you are right*

ralentir *v:* to slow down
ralentir le pas — to slacken one's pace; to slow down

rancart *m:* rubbish, waste
mettre au rancart — throw out; cast aside; get shot of

rancune *f:* grudge, rancour
il me garde rancune — he bears me a grudge

rappeler *v:* to call back, to recall, to remember
cela me rappelle — that puts me in mind of
je ne me rappelle pas l'adresse — I do not remember the address
rappelez-moi à son bon souvenir — give him my kind regards

rapport *m:* connection, relationship, report
par rapport à — with regard to; in comparison with; in relation to
sous tous les rapports — from every point of view; in every respect

rattraper *v:* to recapture, to get back
rattraper le temps perdu — to make up for lost time

ravir *v:* to delight, to ravish
je suis ravi de vous voir — I am delighted to see you
ravi de vous connaître — delighted to meet you; pleased to meet you

réception *f:* reception, party
recevoir du monde; donner une petite réception — to give a party

recevoir *v:* to receive
au reçu de — on receipt of
être reçu à un examen — to pass an examination

je suis reçu

recharger *v:* to recharge
recharger ses accus — to recharge one's batteries; to take a well earned rest

récit *m:* account, story
faire le récit de — to give an account of; to tell the story of

recours *m:* resort, recourse
avoir recours à — to have recourse to; to resort to

91

redire *v:* to say again, to repeat

trouver à redire à quelque chose — *to find fault with something*

réfléchir *v:* to reflect, to think

c'est tout réfléchi — *my mind is made up*

réfléchissez-y! — *think it over!*

réflexion *f:* reflection, thought

à la réflexion; réflexion faite — *on second thoughts*

toute réflexion faite; tout bien considéré — *all things considered*

refuser *v:* to refuse, to decline, to reject

être refusé (à un examen) — *to fail (an examination)*

il vaudrait mieux refuser — *it would be better to refuse*

regarder *v:* to look at, to concern

ça ne vous regarde pas — *it's none of your business*

je le regardais en face — *I looked him in the face*

regarder de travers — *to look askance at; to give a dirty look*

regarder quelqu'un à la dérobée — *to steal a glance at someone; to give someone a surreptitious glance*

regarder quelqu'un de haut en bas — *to look someone up and down*

se regarder en chiens de faïence — *to glare at one another*

y regarder à deux fois avant faire quelque chose — *to think twice before doing something*

régime *m:* regime, diet

être au régime; suivre un régime — *to be on a diet*

régime amaigrissant — *slimming diet*

suivre un régime amaigrissant

règle *f:* rule

il faut faire la demande dans (ou selon) les règles — *you must make your request according to the rules (or proper procedures)*

régler *v:* to settle, to pay, to regulate

j'ai réglé la note — *I have paid the bill*

regretter *v:* to be sorry, to regret

je regrette, mais cette table a déjà été reservée — *I'm sorry, but this table has already been reserved*

je regrette de vous avoir fait attendre — *I'm sorry to have kept you waiting*

relâche *m, f:* respite, rest, closed

le théâtre fait relâche — *the theatre is closed*

sans relâche — *without respite; without ceasing*

remettre *v:* to put back, to postpone

remettre une affaire à plus tard — *to postpone a matter; to let a matter stand over*

remonter *v:* to climb back up, to come back, to wind up, to renew

il est remonté à bloc aujourd'hui — *he's on top form today*

il est remonté, il n'arrête pas de parler — *he's full of vigour and won't stop talking*

je lui ai remonté le moral — *I cheered him up*

remuer *v:* to move

remuer ciel et terre pour — *to move heaven and earth to; to leave no stone unturned to*

rendez-vous *m:* appointment

prendre rendez-vous avec quelqu'un — *to make an appointment with someone; to arrange to see someone*

rendre *v:* to give back, to return, to repay

rendre le bien pour le mal — *to return good for evil*

sans s'en rendre compte — *without realizing it*

renseignement(s) *m, mpl:* information

aller aux renseignements — *to make inquiries*

je peux vous demander un renseignement? — *can you give me some information?*

rentes *fpl:* income

avoir des rentes — *to have a private income*

vivre de ses rentes | to live on (or have) a private income

rentrer v: to go back, to come back, to return

il rentre; il revient chez soi | he's going back home
rentrer les mains vides | to return empty-handed

renvoyer v: to dismiss, to expel, to postpone

être renvoyé | to get the sack
renvoyer (ou remettre) quelque chose aux calendes grecques | to put something off indefinitely

répandre (se) v: to spread, to be spread, to spill

cette opinion se répand | this opinion is gaining ground; this opinion is spreading

réparation f: repair, repairing

la maison est en réparation | the house is under repair

repasser v: to come back, to go back

je repasserai | I'll call in again; I'll come back

passer et repasser | to pass to and fro
repasser à la pattemouille | to iron under a damp cloth

réponse f: reply, response, answer

c'est la réponse du berger à la bergère | it's tit for tat
il a me fait une réponse de Normand | he wouldn't give me a straight answer; he wouldn't say yes or no

reprendre v: to recapture, to catch again, to take up

le problème a été repris par le directeur | the problem has been taken up by the manager
que je vous y reprenne! | let me catch you at it again!

représailles fpl: reprisals

par voie de représailles; en représailles de | by way of reprisal (for)

réserve f: reserve, reservation

se tenir sur la réserve | to be on one's guard; to be reserved about

respect m: respect

présentez mes respects à | give my best regards to

responsabilité f: responsibility

il endosse une responsabilité | he assumes (shoulders) responsibility

reste m: *remainder, rest*

être en reste	*to be in arrears; to be behindhand*
être (ou demeurer) en reste avec quelqu'un	*to be outdone by someone; to be indebted to someone*
n'être jamais en reste	*to be never at lost for words*

rester v: *to stay, to remain*

en rester baba	*to be dumbfounded*
il reste à savoir si	*it remains to be seen whether*
il me reste cinquant francs	*I have fifty francs left*
j'en suis resté baba	*you could have knocked me down with a feather*
ne pas rester sur un refus	*not to take no for an answer*
nous ne pouvons rester que quelques instants	*we can only stay for a few moments*
rester le bec dans l'eau	*to be nonplussed; to be left in the lurch*

retard m: *backwardness*

avoir un métro de retard	*to be very slow on the uptake*

retenir v: *to book, to reserve*

retenir des places	*to book seats*

retomber v: *to fall again, to land, to fall*

tout est retombé sur sa tête	*he was left holding the baby*

retordre v: *to wring out*

donner du fil à retordre	*to give a great deal of trouble; to have one's work cut out*

retour m: *return*

avec faculté de retour	*on approval; on sale or return*
de retour chez moi	*on my return home; back home*
en retour de	*in return for; in exchange for*
il est de retour	*he has returned; he is back again*

retraite f: *retreat, retirement, pension*

prendre sa retraite	*to retire; to go into retirement*
prendre une retraite anticipée	*to retire early; to take early retirement*
toucher (ou percevoir) une petite retraite	*to receive a small pension*

rien

réussir *v:* to succeed, to be a success
à force d'essayer, il a réussi — *by dint of trying he succeeded*

révéler *v:* to reveal, to disclose
se révéler (comme) ambitieux — *to prove to be ambitious; to show oneself to be ambitious*

revendre *v:* to resell
nous en avons à revendre — *we have enough and to spare*

revenir *v:* to come back, to return
mais revenons à nos moutons — *let us return to the subject*
ne revenons pas sur le passé — *let bygones be bygones*
revenir de loin — *to have been touch and go; to have had a close shave*
revenir sur ses pas — *to retrace one's steps*

revenu *m:* income
dépenser tout son revenu — *to live up to one's income; to live beyond one's income*

rêver *v:* to dream
je rêve du jour où cela arrivera — *I can't wait for the day when that happens*

revers *m:* back, reverse
le revers de la medaille — *the other side of the coin; the dark side of the picture*

revoir *v:* to see again, to meet again
ça fait bien plaisir de vous revoir — *it's lovely to see you again*

revue *f:* review
passer en revue — *to review; to review in one's mind; to inspect*

ridicule *adj & m:* ridiculous, ridicule, absurdity
se rendre ridicule aux yeux de tous — *to make a fool of oneself; to make oneself look ridiculous*
tomber dans le ridicule — *to make oneself ridiculous; to become ridiculous*
tourner quelqu'un en ridicule — *to ridicule someone*

rien *pron:* nothing
ça ne fait rien — *it's all right; it doesn't matter*
comme si de rien n'était — *as if nothing had happened*
il n'a été pour rien dans l'affaire — *he has had no hand in the affair; he has had nothing to do with the affair*

il n'y a rien à faire — it can't be helped; there is nothing to be done

pour trois fois rien — for next to nothing; very cheaply

   rien que adv: nothing but, only, merely

rien que d'y penser (ou songer) me fait frissoner — the mere (or very) thought of it makes me shiver

   rigoler v: to laugh, to have fun

il a fait ça pour rigoler — he did it for a giggle

   rire m: laugh, laughter

il n'y a pas de quoi rire — it's no laughing matter

rire étouffé — chuckle; stifled laugh

   rire v: to laugh

il a toujours le mot pour rire — he's always joking; he's a born joker

rire à gorge déployée — to roar with laughter; to laugh outright

rire aux éclats — to roar with laughter

rire dans sa barbe; rire en cachette — to laugh up one's sleeve; to have a quiet laugh

rire jaune — to laugh on the other side of one's face

rire sous cape — to laugh up one's sleeve

   risée f: jeer, derision

être la risée de — to be the laughing stock of

   rôle m: part, role, roll

jouer un rôle — to play a part; to act a role

jouer un rôle prépondérant dans — to play a leading part in; to be the main factor in

quel a été son rôle dans cette affaire? — what part did he play in this business?

   rouler v: to roll

rouler les mécaniques — to swagger; to strut about

rouler par terre — to roll on the ground

rouler toute la nuit — to drive all night

   route f: road, path, way

ils ont fait fausse route — they went the wrong way

nous avons fait route ensemble — we walked along together

97

S

saigner *v:* to bleed

se saigner aux quatre veines;   *to make great sacrifices*
faire de grands sacrifices

saisir *v:* to seize, to take hold of

saisir (ou prendre) la balle   *to seize (or jump at) the*
au bond   *opportunity*

sang *m:* blood

se faire un sang d'encre   *to be worried stiff (or to*
    death)

sang-froid *m:* sangfroid, cool, calm

garder son sang-froid   *to keep calm; to keep one's*
    cool

sanglot *m:* sob

éclater en sanglots   *to burst into sobs (or tears)*

sans *prep:* without

il est sans le sou; il n'a pas   *he is penniless; he is down*
le sou; il est sans ressources   *and out*

sans-gêne *m, f inv:* inconsiderate or unceremonious person

il est un sans-gêne   *he is offhand; he is an*
    inconsiderate type

santé *f:* health

à votre santé!; santé!   *cheers!; good health!*
boire à la santé de quelqu'un   *to drink someone's health*
en mauvaise/bonne santé   *in bad/good health*

saut *m:* jump, leap

faire le saut   *to take the plunge*
il n'y a qu'un saut d'ici   *it's only a stone's throw from*
    here

sauter *v:* to jump, to leap

cela saute aux yeux   *that is quite obvious; that*
    sticks out a mile

sauter à saute-mouton par-   *to leapfrog over (a person)*
dessus

sauter au plafond   *to blow one's top; to raise*
    the roof

sauter de-ci de-là   *to jump about*
sauter le pas; sauter le fossé   *to take the plunge*

sauter sur l'occase	*to jump at the chance; to seize the opportunity*
sauve-qui-peut m, inv:	*stampede, panic, mad rush*
sauve qui peut!	*run for your lives!; each one for him (her) self!*
sauver (se) v: *to escape, to run away*	
il se fait tard, je me sauve	*it's getting late, I must hurry off*
sauver v: *to save, to rescue*	
il m'a sauvé la mise	*he got me out of a tight corner*
pour sauver les apparences	*to keep up appearences*
sauver la situation	*to retrieve the situation*
sauver sa peau	*to save oneself; to save one's skin*
savoir v: *to know*	
c'est à savoir si	*it is a question whether*
être payé pour le savoir	*to know it to one's cost; to learn the hard way*
je ne sais comment m'y prendre	*I don't know how to set about it*
je ne sais trop que faire	*I am not quite sure what to do*
je ne sais trop si	*I am not too sure whether*
pas que je sache	*not as far as I know; not to my knowledge*

je ne sais trop que faire

99

sens

savoir à n'en pas douter que	to know for certain that
savoir vivre	to know how to behave; to know how to live
si j'avais su	had I known; if I had known
savoir-faire m: know-how	
savoir-faire	know-how; ability; tact
savon m: soap	
passer un savon à quelqu'un	to give someone a good ticking-off
scène f: stage	
monter sur la scène	to take to the stage; to become an actor (actress)
scrupule m: scruple	
il ne se fait aucun scrupule	he does not scruple to
secours m: help, assistance	
être d'un grand secours à	to be a great help to
secret m: secret, secrecy	
dans le plus grand secret	with the utmost secrecy
séjourner v: to stay	
j'ai séjourné chez lui	I stayed at his house
selle f: saddle	
être bien en selle	to be firmly in the saddle
sellette f: stool, turntable, stand	
être sur la sellette	to be in the hot seat; to be on the spot
selon prep: according to, in accordance with	
c'est selon	it all depends
vivre selon ses moyens	to live according to one's means
semaine f: week	
la semaine de quatre jeudis	a month of Sundays
semblant m: semblance	
faire semblant de (+inf)	to pretend to (+vb)
sembler v: to seem, to appear to	
si bon vous semble	if you see fit
sens m: sense, meaning, direction	
en dépit du sens commun	against all common sense; any old how
mettre sens dessus dessous	to turn upside down

ce vin sent de — — —

sentir *v:* to feel, to smell, to taste

ce thé sent le citron — this tea smells of lemon; this tea tastes of lemon

sentir (se) *v:* to feel

se sentir patraque — to feel off-colour; to feel a bit under the weather

se sentir un peu chose — to feel a bit off form

série *f:* set, series

hors série — incomparable; specially made; custom made

sérieux *m:* seriousness, reliability

prendre au sérieux — to take seriously

servir *v:* to serve

à quoi sert de (+*inf*) — what good is it to (+*vb*); what would be the point of (+*vb*)

siège *m:* seat

siège arrière — back seat; pillion seat

signe *m:* sign, gesture

faire signe à quelqu'un — to beckon someone; to get in touch with someone

silencieux,-euse *adj:* silent, quiet

rester silencieux — to remain silent

simple *adj:* simple, single

c'est simple comme bonjour (ou chou) — it's dead easy

sitôt *adv:* as soon as

il ne reviendra pas de sitôt! — he wont come back here again in a hurry!

sitôt que; sitôt après — as soon as; no sooner than

soi-disant *adj & adv:* so-called, would-be, supposedly

notre soi-disant poète — our so-called (or would-be) poet

soleil *m:* sun

au coucher du soleil; à soleil couché — at sunset

au lever du soleil — at sunrise

couché en plein soleil — lying full in the sun

recevoir un coup de soleil — to get sunburnt; to get a touch of sunstroke

sourd

solution *f:* solution
il n'y a pas trente-six solutions — *there's only one solution*
somme *m:* nap, snooze
faire un petit somme — *to have forty winks*
sommeil *m:* sleep
avoir le sommeil léger/lourd — *to be a light/heavy sleeper*
avoir sommeil — *to feel sleepy; to be sleepy*
son *m:* sound
c'est un autre son de cloche — *that's another story; that's another way of looking at it*
j'étais réveillé par le son des cloches — *I was woken by the sound of bells*
songer *v:* to dream, to think about
il ne faut pas y songer — *it's out of the question*
sorte *f:* sort, kind
de la sorte — *in such a manner; in that fashion; in that way*
sortir *v:* to go out, to leave
on n'est pas sorti de l'auberge — *we're not out of the wood yet*
sot *m,* **sotte** *f:* fool, idiot
sot achevé — *down-right ass; absolute fool*
soubresaut *m:* start, jolt
La nouvelle m'a donné un soubresaut — *the news gave me a start*
souci *m:* worry
être sans souci — *to be carefree; to have no worries*
souffle *m:* breath, blow, puff
retenir son souffle — *to hold one's breath*
source *f:* source, spring
je le tiens de bonne source — *I got it staight from the horse's mouth*
sourd,-e *adj:* deaf
il est sourd comme un pot — *he is stone deaf; he's as deaf as a post*
faire la sourde oreille à — *to turn a deaf ear to*
sourd-muet; sourde-muette — *deaf-mute; deaf-and-dumb person*

102

sourdine f: mute
faire quelque chose en sourdine — to do something secretly (or on the sly)

souriant,-e adj: smiling, cheerful
elle était toute souriante — she was full of smiles

sourire v: to smile
sourire d'un air satisfait (ou affecté) — to smirk (in a self-satisfied, or affected way)

sous-fifre m: underling, dogsbody, second fiddle
être le sous-fifre de quelqu'un — to play second fiddle to someone

souvenir (se) v: to remember, to recall
autant qu'il m'en souvient — to the best of my recollection
du plus loin qu'il me souvienne — as far back as I can remember
s'il m'en souvient bien — if I remember rightly
souviens-toi de ta promesse! — remember your promise!

souvent adv: often
peu souvent — seldom; infrequently

stop m: stop, halt sign
ils ont fait du stop jusqu'à Paris — they hitch-hiked to Paris

style m: style
style ampoulé — turgid style; pompous style; high-flown style

succès m: success
remporter un vif succès — to achieve great success

suite f: continuation, sequel
à la suite de — as the result of; following
par la suite; dans la suite — subsequently; afterwards

suivre v: to follow
suivez-moi — follow me
suivre les cours (ou classes) — to attend school; to attend a course of studies

supporter v: to support, to withstand, to endure
il peut supporter l'alcool (ou la boisson) — he can hold his liquor (or drink)

supposer v: to suppose, to assume
supposez pour un instant — suppose for argument's sake

tabac

sur *prep:* on
sur-le-champ; sur l'heure | *immediately; at once; straightaway*

sûr,-e *adj:* safe, sure
bien sûr; bien entendu | *of course; surely*
être sûr | *to be assured; to rest assured*

suranné,-e *adj:* outmoded, outdated
être suranné | *to be out-of-date; to be out of fashion*

surcroît *m:* addition, increase
par surcroît; de surcroît | *moreover; what is more*
pour surcroît de malheur | *to make matters worse*

sûreté *f:* safety
pour plus de sûreté | *as an extra precaution; to be on the safe side*

surprendre *v:* to surprise, to catch in the act, to overhear
j'ai surpris une conversation très curieuse | *I've overheard a very strange conversation*
surprendre des amis chez eux | *to pay a surprise visit to friends*

surtout *adv:* above all, especially, particularly
j'aime surtout les romans d'amour | *I particularly like romantic novels*
surtout pas!; certainement pas! | *certainly not!; absolutely not!*
surtout que | *especially as; since*

surveiller *v:* to watch
surveiller quelqu'un de près | *to keep a close eye on someone*

survivre (à) *v:* to outlive, to outlast
elle a survécu à son mari | *she outlived her husband*

sus (en) *adv:* in addition
en sus de | *in addition to; over and above*

T

tabac *m:* tobacco, tobacconist's
faire un tabac | *to be a smash hit; to be a roaring success (entertainment)*

tâche *f:* task, work, job
il est à la hauteur de la tâche — he is up to the task

taille *f:* size, height, measure
grandes/petites/toutes tailles — large/small/all sizes
il était un homme de petite taille — he was a man short in stature
quelle est votre taille? — what size do you take?

tailler *v:* to cut, to carve
elles taillent des bavettes — they gossip; they natter

tant *adv:* so much
il est un tant soit peu réservé — he's ever so slightly reserved; he's a little bit shy

tant bien que mal — as well as possible; after a fashion; so-so

tant pis — never mind; that's too bad
tant s'en faut!; loin de là! — far from it!; not by a long way!

tant que *conj:* as long as, while
tant que je vivrai — as long as I live

tapage *m:* din, uproar, row, fuss
faire du tapage — to create a din; to cause a furore

tapinois *m:* slyboots
en tapinois — slyly; on the sly; furtively

taquiner *v:* to tease
tu me taquine — you are teasing me

elles taillent des bavettes

temps

tard *adv:* late	
au plus tard	at the latest
il commence à se faire tard; il se fait tard	it's getting late
mieux vaut tard que jamais	better late than never
quelques instants plus tard	a few moments later
tarder *v:* to delay	
je ne tarderai guère à m'habiller	I shall not be long in getting dressed
sans tarder	without delay
taux *m:* rate	
au taux de	at the rate of (quantity)
télé *f abb:* telly (TV)	
à la télé	on the telly (TV)
allume la télé, s'il vous plait	turn on the telly (or TV), please
qu'est-ce qu'il y a à la télé ce soir?	what's on the telly (or TV) tonight?
tellement *adv:* so, so much	
il ne travaille pas tellement	he does not work that much
temps *m:* time, weather	
au temps pour moi!	my mistake!
avec le temps; à la longue	with time; in the course of time; as time goes by
cela fait gagner beaucoup de temps	it saves a great deal of time; it's very time-saving
de temps en temps; de temps à autre	from time to time; now and again
en ce temps là	at that time; in those days
en temps et lieu; en son temps	in due course; at the proper time
en temps utile; en temps voulu	at the proper time; in due time; in due course
vous aurez tout votre temps	you will have all the time in the world (or all the time you need)
vous avez juste le temps de	you have just time to; you have just long enough to

106

tenir *v:* to hold, to adhere, to keep

avoir de qui tenir	to be a chip off the old block; to be of good stock
tenir quelqu'un compagnie	to keep someone company
ils se tenaient par la main	they were holding hands
qu'à cela ne tienne	never mind that; that's no problem
se tenir coi; rester coi	to remain silent; to lie low
tenez-vous bien!; tiens-toi bien!	wait for it!
tenir à distance	to keep at a distance (or arm's length)
tenir bon; tenir ferme	to hold out; to stand fast; to hold one's ground
tenir le bon bout	to have the matter well in hand; to be past the worse
tenir table ouverte	to keep open house
tenir tête à l'orage; braver l'orage	to face the music
tenir un chien en laisse	to keep a dog on a lead

tenir (se) *v:* to hold on to, to be standing

se tenir (ou se dresser) sur la pointe des pieds	to stand on tiptoe

tenue *f:* upkeep, dress, quality

en grande tenue	in full dress; in full uniform
en tenue negligée	carelessly dressed; scruffily dressed
en tenue soirée	in evening dress
être en tenue décontractée	to wear casual clothes
une tenue passe-partout	a general (or all) purpose outfit (clothes)

terme *m:* term, word

dans toute la force du terme	in the full sense of the word
en d'autres termes	in other words

tête *f:* head

à tête reposée	at one's leisure
avoir la tête près du bonnet	to be quick-tempered
de la tête aux pieds	from head to foot; from top to toe
en avoir par-dessus la tête	to be fed up to the back teeth

107

tomber

il a la forte tête	*he is strong-minded*
il n'en fait qu'à sa tête	*he has it all his own way; he does as he pleases*
ne plus savoir où donner de la tête	*not to know which way to turn*
se mettre dans la tête de	*to take it into one's head to*
se mettre martel en tête	*to worry oneself sick; to get worked up*
se tenir sur sa tête	*to stand on one's head*

tirer *v: to draw, to pull, to shoot*

cela ne tire pas à conséquence	*that is of no consequence*
être tiré à quatre épingles	*to be dressed to the nines; to be dressed to kill*
se faire tirer l'oreille	*to need a lot of persuading; to drag one's heels*
tirer à sa fin	*to be drawing to a close; to run low*
tirer au sort	*to draw lots*
tirer le meilleur parti de	*to make the best of*
tirer parti de	*to turn to good account; to take advantage of*
tirer son épingle du jeu	*to get out while the going is good; to play one's game well*
tirer une affaire au clair	*to clear up an affair*

tirer (se) *v: to come through, to come off, to get out of*

s'en bien tirer	*to come off well; to get off lightly*
se tirer d'embarras	*to get out of a difficulty; to get out of trouble*

toilette *f: clothes, dress*

elle fait sa toilette	*she is washing and dressing; she is getting ready*
elle porte bien la toilette	*she wears her clothes well*

tombeau *m: tomb, grave*

à tombeau ouvert	*at breakneck speed*
je serai un vrai tombeau	*my lips are sealed*

tomber *v: to fall*

cela tombe sous le sens	*it's obvious; it's self-evident; it stands to reason*

il n'est pas tombé de la dernière pluie	he's no innocent; he wasn't born yesterday
je suis tombé sur mon viel ami	I ran into my old friend
tomber à la renverse	to fall backwards
tomber à pic (ou à point)	to come at just the right time
tomber de Charybde en Scylla	to jump out of the frying-pan into the fire
tomber de haut	to be badly let down; to be taken aback
tomber de tout son long	to fall full length
tomber d'inanition	to feel faint with hunger
tomber du ciel	to be a godsend; to be heaven sent
tomber des nues	to stand aghast; to be taken aback
tomber sur quelqu'un à bras raccourcis*	to pitch into someone
toqué,-e adj: crazy, cracked, nuts	
être toqué de quelqu'un*	to be crazy (or mad) about someone*
torchon m: duster, tea towel	
donner un coup de torchon (sur)	to give a room a dust; to give the dishes a wipe
le torchon brûle	it's a "daggers drawn" situation
un coup de torchon; un coup de balai	a clean sweep
un coup de torchon; une bagarre	a scrap; a dust-up
tort m: fault, wrong	
à tort ou à raison	rightly or wrongly
donner tort à quelqu'un	to lay the blame on someone
tôt adv: early, soon	
au plus tôt; le plus tôt	at the earliest; as soon as
le plus tôt possible	as soon as possible; as early as possible
le plus tôt sera le mieux	the sooner the better
tôt ou tard	sooner or later
une heure plus tôt	an hour earlier

toucher *v:* to touch, to broach

toucher du bois	to touch wood
toucher un mot à quelqu'un	to have a word with someone; to drop a hint to someone

toujours *adv:* always, still

comme toujours	as always
toujours est-il que	the fact remains that

tour *m:* tour, trick, trip, turn

il a acquis le tour de main pour faire	he has found the knack of doing
c'est le tour classique	it's the oldest trick in the book

tournant *m:* bend

rattraper quelqu'un au tournant	to get one's own back on somebody

tournée *f:* tour

faire la tournée des grands ducs	to have a night out; to go out on a spree

tourner *v:* to turn, to go round, to spin

elle tourne autour du pot	she beats about the bush
faire tourner une pièce de monnaie	to spin a coin

petanque

tout,-e, tous, toutes *adj & adv:* all, every, very

à tout propos	at every opportunity
tous les jours je sors faire des courses	every day I go out shopping
tout à coup; tout d'un coup	suddenly
tout au moins/tout au plus	at the very least/at the very most
tout de suite	immediately; at once

tout à fait *adv:* quite, entirely, altogether

je suis tout à fait d'accord	I'm completely in agreement
tu as fini ton travail? pas tout à fait!	have you finished your work? not completely! (or not quite!)

tout de même *adv:* all the same, even so, quite, really

c'est tout de même étonnant!	it's quite surprising!
tout de même j'essayerai de venir	all the same I shall try to come

tout le monde *pron:* everybody

tout le monde sait cela!   *everybody knows that!*

traduire *v:* to translate

traduire mot à mot   *to translate word for word*

train *m:* train, pace

aller grand train   *to make brisk progress; to move at a great rate*

être en train de faire quelque chose   *to be in the middle of doing something; to be busy doing something*

il est en train   *he is in good form; he is in good spirits*

traiter *v:* to treat, to call

il m'a traité de menteur   *he called me a liar*

traiter quelqu'un de haut en bas   *to treat some one with disdain; to look down on someone*

tranquille *adj:* peaceful, quiet, calm

soyez tranquille, tout ira bien   *don't worry, everything will be all right*

travailler *v:* to work

il travaille comme quatre   *he works like a horse*

travailler ferme; travailler dur   *to work hard*

travailler par accès; travailler par à-coups   *to work by fits and starts*

travailler pour le roi de Prusse   *to work for nothing; to get nothing out of it*

tremper *v:* to soak, to drench

trempé jusqu'aux os   *drenched to the skin*

trente *adj & m:* thirty

être sur son trente et un   *to be wearing one's glad rags; to be dressed to kill*

tous les trente-six du mois   *once in a blue moon*

tromper *v:* to deceive, to mislead, to be unfaithful

cela ne trompe personne   *that doesn't fool anybody*

c'est un signe qui ne trompe pas   *it's a clear sign; it's clear proof*

tromper (se) *v:* to be mistaken

il n'y a pas à s'y tromper   *there is no doubt about it*

je m'étais sûrement trompé   *I must have made a mistake*

si je ne me trompe	*unless I am mistaken*
trop *adv:* too much	
c'en est trop!	*that's the last straw!; that's going too far!*
être de trop	*to be out of place; to be unwanted; to be unwelcome*
je ne sais pas trop	*I don't know exactly*
trotte *f:* distance, stretch	
ça fait une trotte d'ici	*it's quite a way from here; it's a fair distance from here*
trottoir *m:* pavement	
faire le trottoir	*to solicit in the streets; to walk the streets*
trouvaille *f:* find, innovation	
j'ai fait une trouvaille au magasin d'antiquités	*I've made a find at the antique shop*
trouver *v:* to find	
c'est bien trouvé	*that's a good one; that's a happy thought*
c'est tout trouvé	*it's quite simple; it's quite straightforward*
trouver à qui parler	*to meet one's match*
trouver bon de	*to see fit to*
trouver le joint	*to come up with a solution; to find a way*
trouver (se) *v:* to be, to feel, to happen	
il se trouve que j'étais là	*it so happens that I was there; I happened to be there*
je me trouve très bien ici	*I feel quite (or very) comfortable here*
truc *m:* trick, knack, thingummy	
avoir le truc	*to have the knack*
tuer *v:* to kill	
tuer la poule aux oeufs d'or	*to kill the goose that lays the golden eggs*
tué sur le coup	*killed on the spot; killed outright*

U

un, une *indef. art., pron:* a, an, one

c'est tout un
> *it amounts to one and the same thing; it's all the same*

usage *m:* use, custom

c'est l'usage
> *it's the custom; it's the way things are done*

il est d'usage de (+inf)
> *it is customary to*

V

vacances *fpl:* holiday, vacation

nous prenons nos vacances en France
> *we are taking our holiday in France*

partir en vacances
> *to go (away) on holiday*

valoir *v:* to be worth

ça ne vaut pas un clou
> *it's utterly worthless*

cela vaut la peine d'essayer
> *it's worthwhile trying*

il vaut son pesant d'or
> *it is worth its weight in gold*

vaille que vaille
> *come what may; after a fashion; somehow*

valoir le coup
> *to be worth the trouble*

veine *f:* vein

avoir de la veine
> *to be lucky; to have a winning streak*

vendre *v:* to sell

vendre/acheter au comptant
> *to sell/buy for cash*

venir *v:* to come

d'où vient que?
> *how comes that?; what is the reason that?*

en venir au fait
> *to come to the point*

je viendrai vous chercher à sept heures
> *I'll call for you at seven o'clock*

merci d'être venue
> *thank you for coming*

venir à bout de
> *to manage to; to get through; to overcome*

venir/aller à l'aide de
> *to come/go to the help of*

venir v **de:** to have just
elle venait de se lever — she had just got up

vent m: wind
c'est du vent! — it's just hot air!
être dans le vent — to be trendy
il a le vent en poupe — he has the wind in his sails

vérité f: truth
avoir l'accent de la vérité — to ring true
dire la vérité — to speak the truth
en vérité — really; actually

verser v: to pour, to be skilled
il est très versé dans ces matières — he is very experienced in these matters
verser (ou jeter) de l'huile sur le feu — to add fuel to the fire (or flames)

veste f: jacket
ramasser (ou prendre) une veste — to come a cropper; to fall flat on one's face
remporter une veste — to suffer a setback

vie f: life
faire la vie — to live it up; to make a scene; to kick up a row
jamais de la vie! — not on your life!; never!
sa vie ne tient qu'à un fil — his life hangs by a thread

vigueur f: vigour, strength
le règlement est actuellement en vigueur — the regulation is now in force

vite adv: fast, quickly
au plus vite; le plus vite possible — as quickly as possible

vivant m: lifetime, (pl) the living
de son vivant — in his lifetime

vivre v: to live
qui vivra verra — only time will tell
vivre au jour le jour — to live from hand to mouth
vivre au sein du luxe — to live in the lap of luxury
vivre aux crochets de quelqu'un — to live off someone; to sponge off someone
vivre selon ses moyens — to live within one's means

vogue f: fashion, vogue
être en vogue — to be in fashion; to be fashionable

voie f: way
en voie de guérison — on the way to recovery
voile f: sail
mettre à la voile; faire voile — to set sail; to get under sail
voir v: to see
attendez voir — let's see; let's think; wait and see

c'est bien vu? — is that quite clear?; is that understood?

c'est du jamais vu! — you've never seen the like!
c'est tout vu — it's a foregone conclusion
il voit tout en beau; il voit tout en rose — he sees the bright side of everything
il voit tout en noir — he sees the dark side of everything

il y a un siècle qu'on ne vous a vu — I haven't seen you for ages
je te vois venir — I can see what you are getting at

ni vu ni connu! — mum's the word!
on aura tout vu! — that's unbelievable!; I'd never have believed it!

on verra de quel bois je me chauffe! — they'll see what I'm made of!

voir la vie en rose — to see life through rose-coloured spectacles

voix f: voice, vote
elle a parlé à voix voilée — she spoke in a husky voice
mettre la question aux voix — to put the question to the vote

parler d'une voix entrecoupée — to speak in a broken voice
sa voix a un timbre si doux — her voice sounds so sweet
vol m: flight
à vol d'oiseau — as the crow flies
voler v: to fly, to steal
voler en éclats — to fly to pieces; to be shattered

115

volontiers *adv:* willingly, gladly, readily

assez volontiers	readily enough
on croit volontiers que	one is apt to think that

vôtre *pron:* yours, your own

à la bonne vôtre!	your very good health!; cheers!

vôtres *mpl, fpl:* your family, your folk

bonne année à vous et tous les vôtres	Happy New Year to you and yours

vouloir *v:* to want, to wish, to expect

que voulez-vous?	what can you expect?
que voulez-vous que j'y fasse?	what do you expect me to do about it?
vouloir bien	to be willing; to be happy

vouloir *v* **dire:** to mean, to signify

qu'est-ce que cela veut dire?	what does that mean?; what does that imply?

vous *pron:* you

de vous à moi	between you and me; between ourselves

voyage *m:* voyage, trip

partir en voyage	to set out on a journey

vrai *m:* truth; **vrai,-e** *adj:* true, real

c'est pour de vrai?	do you really mean it?
c'est trop beau pour être vrai	it is too good to be true
pour de vrai	for real; really; seriously

vraiment *adv:* really, definitely

je ne sais vraiment pas quoi faire	I really do not know what to do
vous trouvez? oui, vraiment	do you think so? yes definitely

vraisemblablement *adv:* likely, probably, very likely

vraisemblablement	most likely; very likely
vraisemblablement pas	probably not

vue *f:* sight, eyesight, view

à perte de vue	as far as the eye can see; interminably
à vue de nez	at a rough guess; by rule of thumb
avoir des vues sur	to have designs on

être très en vue	to be very much in the public eye
il a la vue basse (ou courte)	he is short-sighted (or near-sighted)
je l'ai perdu de vue	I lost sight of it
vue à vol d'oiseau	bird's-eye view

Y

yeux mpl: *eyes (see also œil)*

avoir les yeux plus grands que le ventre	to bite off more than one can chew
n'avoir pas froid aux yeux	to have pluck
n'avoir plus que ses yeux pour pleurer	to have lost everything; to be left with nothing
ne pas avoir les yeux dans sa poche	to keep one's eyes open
ouvrir de grands yeux	to look surprised; to stare in amazement

Z

zig ou **zigue** m: *guy, fellow, chap*

bon zigue*; bon zig*	a nice bloke*; a decent fellow

zouave m: *clown, comedian*

faire le zouave	to play the fool; to fool around

ENGLISH-FRENCH PHRASES

A

je fais de mon mieux

ability: *capacité f, compétence f*	
as far as I am able; to the best of my ability	*dans la mesure de mes forces (ou capacités)*
to do something to the best of one's ability	*faire quelque chose de son mieux*
able (be): *pouvoir v*	
there's nothing one can do about it; it cannot be helped	*on n'y peut rien*
abroad: *étranger m, extérieur m*	
at home and abroad; inside and outside	*à l'intérieur et à l'extérieur*
he has gone abroad	*il est allé à l'étranger*
accept: *accepter v*	
to accept without fuss	*accepter sans façon*
according to: *d'après adv, selon adv*	
according to him (or her); in his (or her) opinion	*d'après lui (ou elle)*
it all depends	*c'est selon*
to live according to one's means	*vivre selon ses moyens*
account: *compte m*	
to take into account	*tenir compte de*
to take little account of	*faire bon marché de; faire peu de cas de*
acquaint: *aviser v*	
to acquaint oneself with the situation	*se mettre au courant (ou au fait) de la situation*
acquaintance: *connaissance f*	
to strike up an acquaintance with someone	*lier connaissance avec quelqu'un*
acquire: *acquérir v, prendre v*	
to acquire a taste (or liking) for	*prendre goût à*
act: *agir v*	
to act with only the most honourable intentions	*agir en tout bien, tout honneur*

Pinto → je montrais sur la scène

actor, actress: *acteur m, actrice f*

to take to the stage; to become   *monter sur la scène*
an actor (actress)

add: *ajouter v*

to add fuel to the fire (or flames)   *verser de l'huile sur le feu*

addition: *surcroît m, de plus adv, en sus adv*

additional work; extra work   *un surcroît de travail*

in addition to; over and above   *en sus de*

in addition; what is more;   *par surcroît; de surcroît*
moreover

address: *adresser v*

to offer up a prayer to God   *adresser une prière à Dieu*

admire: *admirer v;* **admiration:** *admiration f*

she is admired by every one   *elle fait l'admiration de tous*

admit: *admettre v, avouer v*

to admit one's guilt   *s'avouer coupable*

it must be admitted that   *il faut bien dire que*

advance: *avancer v*

to move forward in fits and   *avancer par saccades*
starts

advantage: *avantage m, profit m*

don't let anyone tread on your   *ne te laisse pas marcher sur*
toes; don't let anyone take   *les pieds*
advantage of you

to have an advantage over   *avoir un avantage sur*
someone   *quelqu'un*

to turn to account (or advantage)   *mettre à profit*

advertisement: *annonce f*

you've tried the small ads?   *vous avez essayé les petites*
(or classified advertisements)?   *annonces?*

advice: *conseil m*

I need some advice on   *j'ai besoin d'un conseil au*
   sujet de

I would like some advice   *je voudrais vous demander*
   conseil

advise: *conseiller v, aviser v*

it is advisable to   *il est conseillé de*

well/ill advised   *bien/mal avisé*

afford: *avoir v les moyens*

I cannot afford it   *je n'en ai pas les moyens*

120

afraid (be): *avoir v peur*

do not be afraid   *n'ayez pas peur*

after: *après prep*

afterwards; after the event   *après coup*

after all: *au demeurant adv*

after all; for all that; in fact;   *au demeurant*
all things considered

a good man all things con-   *un brave homme au*
sidered   *demeurant*

afterwards: *après adv, ensuite adv, plus tard adv*

subsequently; afterwards   *par la suite; dans la suite*

again: *de nouveau adv*

not you again!   *encore vous!*

to do something again; to repeat   *faire quelque chose de*
something once again (or once   *nouveau (ou une fois de*
more)   *plus ou encore une fois)*

age: *âge m*

he is old enough to look after   *il est d'âge à se conduire*
himself

he won't live long; he won't live   *il ne fera pas de vieux os*
to an old age

middle-aged   *entre deux âges*

she is my prop in old age   *elle est mon bâton de*
    vieillesse

the awkward age; the difficult   *l'âge ingrat*
age

to look one's age; to show one's   *accuser son âge*
age

ago: *il y a*

that was ages ago; that was   *il y a belle lurette*
donkey's years ago

agree: *accorder v, se mettre v d'accord*

all agreed that   *tous sont tombés d'accord*
    que

don't you agree?   *vous n'êtes pas d'accord?*

I agree (or grant) that I was   *je vous l'accorde j'avais tort*
wrong

that's agreed; that's understood   *c'est bien entendu*

to agree on   *se mettre d'accord sur*

to agree with   *être d'accord avec*

agreement: *accord m*

O.K.!; agreed! *d'accord!*

to come to an agreement with someone *s'arranger avec quelqu'un*

aim: *but m*

for that (or this) purpose; with this aim in view *dans ce but*

air: *air m*

it's just hot air! *c'est du vent!*

to air a room *donner de l'air à une chambre*

alike (be): *se ressembler v*

they are alike in everything; they are as thick as thieves *ce sont deux têtes sous le même bonnet*

alike: *pareil,-eille adj*

there are no two alike (or the same) *il n'y en pas deux pareils*

all: *tout, toute, tous, toutes adj*

for all that *pour autant*

on the whole; all in all *à tout prendre*

allowance: *allocation f, pension f*

living allowance; alimony (or maintenance) allowance *pension alimentaire*

all right: *ça va, tout va bien*

if you do not mind; if that's all right by you *si cela ne vous dérange pas*

it's all right; it doesn't matter *ça ne fait rien*

almost: *presque adv*

I almost succeeded *j'ai failli réussir*

to almost (+vb) (e.g. fall, die) *manquer de (+inf) (ex. tomber, mourir)*

altogether: *complètement adv*

altogether; well and truly *bel et bien*

always: *toujours adv*

as always *comme toujours*

ambitious: *ambitieux,-euse adj*

to be ambitious; to be hungry for success *avoir les dents longues*

amount: *montant m, total m*

to the amount of; not exceeding; to the extent of *jusqu'à concurrence de*

122

anger: en colère *f*, fureur *f*, fâcher *v*
now you are angry!   *maintenant, tu es fâché!*
to be beside onself with anger   *être hors de soi en colère*
to get angry   *se mettre en colère*
to get thoroughly angry; to blow   *se fâcher tout rouge*
one's top

answer: *réponse f*
he wouldn't give me a straight   *il a me fait une réponse de*
answer; he wouldn't say yes   *Normand*
or no

antique: *objet m antique, ancien m*
to be in the antique trade; to sell   *faire (dans) l'ancien*
antiques

anxiety: *inquiétude f*
there is cause (or good reason)   *il y a lieu d'être inquiet*
for anxiety

anyhow: *n'importe comment*
done any old how; scamped   *fait à la diable*
work

anyone: *quiconque pron, quelqu'un pron*
I know that better than anyone   *je le sais mieux que*
    quiconque

anything: *quelque chose f*
anything-else madam? (in shop)   *et avec ça, madame?*

apologize: *s'excuser v*
to apologize; to offer one's   *faire des excuses; présenter*
apologies   *ses excuses*

apology (due): *amende f honorable*
to make amends; to make a full   *faire amende honorable*
apology

apparently: *apparemment adv, en apparence adv*
apparently, seemingly, on the   *en apparence*
face of it

appeal: *plaire v à, attirer v, appel m*
that appeals to me   *ça me dit*
that doesn't appeal to me very   *ça ne m'enchante beaucoup*
much
to appeal to; to call on; to   *faire appel à*
require

appearance: *apparence f, aspect m, apparition f, arrivée f*

to all appearances; in all probability · *selon toute apparence*

to put in an appearance · *faire acte de présence*

apply: *s'adresser v*

to apply to the proper person · *s'adresser à qui de droit*

appointment: *rendez-vous m, inv*

to make an appointment with someone; to arrange to see someone · *prendre rendez-vous avec quelqu'un*

approval: *approbation f*

on approval · *à condition; sous condition; à l'essai*

aptitude: *dispositions fpl*   je n'ai pas

to have an aptitude (or gift) for · *avoir des dispositions pour* jouer de pian

arm: *bras m*

arm in arm · *bras dessus, bras dessous*

he put his arm out of joint · *il s'est démis le bras*

arrears: *arriéré m*

to be in arrears; to be behindhand · *être en reste*

arrive: *arriver v*

to burst in; to breeze in · *arriver en coup de vent*

as far as: *autant que adv*

as far as I know; to the best of my knowledge · autant que je sache

ask: *demander v*

I ask nothing better; that's just what I'd like · *je ne demande pas mieux*

to ask point-blank · *demander à brûle-pourpoint*

as much as: *autant que adv*

as much as possible; as far as possible · autant que possible

assail: *assaillir v*

to demolish a theory; to assail a theory · *battre en breche une théorie*

assume: *admettre v*

granted that; assuming that; supposing that · *en admettant que*

assure: affirmer v, assurer v
to be assured; to rest assured   être sûr
astonish: étonner v
the astonishing thing is that   ce qu'il y a d'étonnant, c'est que

j'ai suivi les cours

attend: être v à, suivre v
to attend school; to attend a   suivre les cours (ou classes)
course of studies

de français

auction: enchères fpl
to put up for auction   mettre aux enchères
authority: autorité f
to have authority to   avoir qualité pour
average: moyenne f, moyen,-enne adj
on (an) average   en moyenne
the average man; the man in   l'homme moyen
the street
aversion: aversion f
that is my pet aversion (or pet   c'est ma bête noire
hate)
await: attendre v
to await events; to sit tight   attendre les événements

B

baby: bébé m
he was left holding the baby   tout est retombé sur sa tête
back: dos m
get off my back!; leave me in   lâche-moi les baskets!*
peace!
background: ombre f, fond m
to keep in the background   se tenir (ou rester) dans
l'ombre

bad: mal adj
never mind; that's too bad   tant pis
to be on bad terms with   être mal avec quelqu'un
somebody; to be in someone's
bad books

bag: *sac m*

it's in the bag; the deal is all sewn up — *l'affaire est dans le sac*

band: *musique f, orchestre m*

strike up the band!; let's get going!; off we go! — *en avant la musique!*

bankrupt: *failli,-e adj & m,f;* **bankruptcy:** *banqueroute f, faillite f*

to be bankrupt — *être en faillite*

to go bankrupt — *faire faillite; faire banqueroute*

barely: *juste adj & adv*

only just; hardly; barely; exactly — *tout juste*

bargain: *marché m, occasion f*

into the bargain; on top of all that — *par-dessus le marché*

to make (or strike) a good bargain — *faire un marché avantageux*

what a bargain! — *quelle occasion!*

bark: *aboiement m, aboi m*

someone whose bark is worse than their bite — *un dur au cœur tendre*

basically: *au fond adv*

basically; in fact; at heart — *au fond; dans le fond*

be: *être v*

that being the case — *cela étant*

where have you been? — *où avez-vous été?*

bean: *haricot m*

not to have a bean left — *n'avoir plus un radis (ou le sou)*

beat: *battre v*

she beats about the bush — *elle tourne autour du pot*

to beat hollow; to beat hands down — *battre à plate couture*

to get beaten at the post — *se faire coiffer au poteau*

because of: *en raison de prep*

on account of; because of; owing to — *à cause de*

bed: *lit m*

to get out of bed on the wrong side — *se lever du pied gauche*

before: *avant prep*
before coming to see you — *avant de venir vous voir*
before long; shortly — *avant peu*

beg: *solliciter v*
to sit up and beg (dog); to curry favour — *faire le beau*

believe: *croire v*
I have every reason to believe that — *j'ai toutes les raisons de croire que*
it's unbelievable!; it's beyond belief! — *c'est à n'y pas croire!*
there is every reason to believe — *il y a tout lieu de croire que*
you can only believe half of what he says — *il faut en prendre et en laisser*

bend: *coude m*
to drive someone round the bend (or up the wall) — *faire tourner quelqu'un en bourrique*

be necessary: *falloir v*
I have to leave; I must leave; it is necessary for me to leave — *il faut que je parte*

best: *meilleur,-e adj*
and the best part of it is that — *et le plus fort, c'est que*
to make the best of — *tirer le meilleur parti de*

better (to get the): *triompher v*
to get the better of someone — *avoir raison de quelqu'un; triompher de quelqu'un*

better: *meilleur,-e adj, mieux adj & adv*
all the better; even better — *d'autant mieux*
he is better — *il se porte mieux; il va mieux*
he's no better off; he's no further on — *il n'en est pas plus avancé*
I know that better than anybody — *je le sais mieux que quiconque*
it's better and better — *c'est de plus en plus fort*
so much the better; that's fine — *tant mieux*
to get the better of; to have the upper hand — *avoir le dessus sur*

between: *entre prep*
between two people; privately — *entre quatre yeux*

between you and me; between ourselves	*de vous à moi*
beyond: *au delà adv*	
beyond that is the river	*au delà il y a la rivière*
bias: *parti m pris, préjugé m*	
to be biased	*être de parti pris*
to take an unbiased view	*juger sans parti pris*
bird: *oiseau m*	
a little bird told me	*mon petit doigt me l'a dit*
to kill two birds with one stone	*faire d'une pierre deux coups*
bit: *morceau m*	
and a bit more (besides)!	*et le pouce!*
bit: *mors m (cheval)*	
he took the bit between his teeth	*il a pris le mors aux dents*
bite: *bouchée f, morceau m*	
not to have a bite to eat	*n'avoir rien à se mettre sous la dent*
bite: *piquer v, mordre v*	
what has bitten you?	*quelle mouche t'a piqué?*
bite off: *arracher v d'un coup de dents*	
to bite off more than one can chew	*avoir les yeux plus grands que le ventre*
blame: *faute f, responsabilité f*	
to lay the blame on someone	*donner tort à quelqu'un*
to lay the blame on	*faire retomber la faute sur*
blink (machine): *être v détraqué*	
to be on the blink; to be giving out	*battre la breloque (appareil)*
blow, stroke: *coup m*	
to give the finishing stroke to; to give the death blow	*donner le coup de grâce à*
to take it; to keep a stiff upper lip; to withstand the blow	*tenir le coup*
blow up (explode): *exploser v, sauter v*	
to blow one's top; to raise the roof	*sauter au plafond*
blues: *le cafard*	
to have the blues; to be down in the dumps	*avoir le cafard*

bold: *hardi,-e* adj

to put on a bold front;
to swagger

faire le brave

bone: *os* m

he made no bones about telling
him; he didn't mind telling him

*il ne s'est pas gêné pour le lui
dire*

I have a bone to pick with you

j'ai maille à partir avec toi

book: *réserver* v, *retenir* v

to book seats

*réserver des places; retenir
des places*

book: *livre* m

to be in the good books of

être dans les petits papiers de

boost: *faire* v *du battage*

to boost; to push; to sing the
praises of

faire l'article

bore: *ennuyer* v   On peut

to be bored to tears

∧ *mourir d'ennui*

to bore someone stiff; to wear
someone out; to get on
someone's nerves

casser les pieds à quelqu'un

born (to be): *naître* v

to be born under a lucky star

être né sous une bonne étoile

to be born with a silver spoon in
one's mouth; to be born lucky

être né coiffé

to stem from; to be descended
from; to be born of

être issu de

boss: *mener* v

to boss around; to have under
one's thumb

mener à la baguette

bottom: *fond* m

from top to bottom; completely

de fond en comble

→ **brainwave:** *idée* f *de génie*   C'est une idée

he has had a brilliant idea (or
brainwave)

il a eu l'idée lumineuse

brazen: *crâner* v

we must brazen it out

il faut payer d'effronterie

break: *manquer* v *à*

to break one's word

*manquer à sa parole (ou
promesse)*

break: *pause f*

to have a coffee break	*faire une pause café*

breath: *haleine f, souffle m*

all in one breath	*tout d'une haleine*
to hold one's breath	*retenir son souffle*
to recover one's breath; to take a breather	*reprendre haleine*

breather: *moment m de répit*

to go out for a breather	*prendre un bol d'air*

bride and groom: *les accordés mpl, les mariés mpl*

the bride and bridegroom are overjoyed	*les accordés (ou les mariés) sont tout heureux*

bring round: *amener v*

I brought the conversation round to another subject	*j'ai amené la conversation sur un autre sujet*

brisk: *vif adj, rapide adj*

to make brisk progress; to move at a great rate	*aller grand train*

broadly: *en gros m*

by and large (or broadly) this question is settled	*cette question est résolue en gros*

broke: *fauché adj*

to be broke	*être fauché comme les blés*

build: *bâtir v, construire v*

to build castles in the air; to build castles in Spain	*bâtir (ou faire) des châteaux en Espagne*

to build castles in the air

    burst: *éclater v*

to burst out laughing   *éclater de rire*

    business: *affaire f, affaires fpl*

enough said, let's get down to   *(c'est) assez causé!*
business!

it's my business, not yours   *c'est mon affaire, non la*
                                   tienne

mind your own business   *mêlez-vous de ce qui vous*
                                   regarde

that's none of your business   *ça ne vous regarde pas*

to get down to business   *passer aux choses sérieuses*

to proceed to the business of   *passer à l'ordre du jour*
the day

    busy: *occupé,-e adj*

I am very busy at present   *je suis très occupé en ce*
                                   moment

I have had a busy week   *j'ai passé une semaine*
                                   chargée

to be as busy as a bee; to be   *faire la mouche du coche*
fussing around; to be a busybody

    buy: *acheter v*

he has bought a pig in a poke   *il a acheté chat en poche*

to buy something on credit   *acheter quelque chose à*
                                   crédit

    bygones: *passé m*

let bygones be bygones   *ne revenons pas sur le passé*

C

    cake: *gâteau m*

it's a piece of cake; it's a doddle *c'est du gâteau*

to want to have one's cake and   *vouloir le beurre et l'argent*
eat it   *du beurre*

    call: *appeler v, aller voir v, passer voir v*

he called me a liar   *il m'a traité de menteur*

to call a spade a spade   *appeler un chat un chat*

to call for help   *appeler au secours*

to call on someone   *passer chez quelqu'un*

we must call the doctor   *il faut appeler le docteur*

care: *se soucier v, soin m*

he couldn't care less about it	*il s'en fiche pas mal*
I don't care a rap; I don't care a damn!	*je m'en bats l'œil*
I don't care that much!; I don't give a damn!	*je m'en fiche!*
I don't care two pins about it	*je m'en moque comme de l'an quarante*
I don't mind; I don't care either way	*ça m'est égal*

carry: *porter v*

to carry coals to Newcastle	*porter de l'eau à la rivière (ou à la mer)*
to carry the can	*porter le chapeau*
to carry something over the shoulder	*porter quelque chose en bandoulière*

carry out: *exécuter v, réaliser v*

to carry out a plan	*mettre un projet à exécution*

cart: *charrette f*

to put the cart before the horse	*mettre la charrue devant les bœufs*

case: *cas m*

if the case arises; if need be	*le cas échéant*
in case of need; if need be	*en cas de besoin*
in such a case	*en pareil cas*

casual clothes: *vêtements mpl sport inv*

to wear casual clothes	*être en tenue décontractée*
in casuals	*en vêtements sport*
sportswear	*vêtements de sport*

cat: *chat m*

they lead a cat and dog life	*ils s'accordent comme chien et chat*
to be like a cat on hot bricks	*se démener comme un diable dans un bénitier*
to let the cat out of the bag; to give the game away	*vendre la mèche; éventer la mèche*

catch: *attraper v, prendre v*

he was caught in the act	*il a été pris sur le fait*
I've caught a cold	*j'ai attrapé un rhume*
let me catch them at it!	*si je les y prends!*

to catch someone red-handed	*prendre quelqu'un la main dans le sac*
catch again: *reprendre* v	
let me catch you at it again!	*que je vous y reprenne!*
ceremony: *cérémonie* f	
he stands on ceremony	*il fait des cérémonies*
certainly: *certainement* adv	
certainly not!; absolutely not!	*surtout pas!; certainement pas!*
chance: *chance* f	
by chance; at random	*par hasard*
randomly; aimlessly; at a guess	*au hasard*
to take one's chance; to try one's luck	*courir la chance*
change: *changement* m, *changer* v	
a change for the better	*un changement en bien (ou en mieux)*
that changes everything; that makes all the difference	*cela change tout!*
to change one's mind (or opinion)	*changer d'avis; changer d'idée*
change: *monnaie* f	
I have no change	*je n'ai pas de monnaie*
small change	*petite monnaie*
chap: *type* m	
he's a decent sort (or fellow)	*c'est un brave type*
charming: *charmant,-e* adj	
he is a charming man to work with	*c'est un collaborateur charmant*
she is more charming than ever	*elle est plus charmante que jamais*
chat: *bavarder* v	
to chat someone up; to toady up to someone	*faire du plat à quelqu'un*
cheap: *bon marché* adj, inv	
I bought all my books cheaply	*j'ai acheté tous mes livres à bon marché*
to buy at a cheap rate; to buy cheap	*acheter à bon compte*

handwritten margin notes: je peux/chois courir la chance; vous avez de monnaie?; vous êtes

133

cheer (up): *prendre v courage, prendre v espoir*

I cheered him up — *je lui ai remonté le moral*

children: *enfants m, fpl*

little children; young children — *les enfants en bas âge*

chip: *éclat m*

he's a chip off the old block — *c'est bien le fils de son père*

to be a chip off the old block; — *avoir de qui tenir*
to be of good stock

to be a chip off the old block; — *chasser de race*
to run in the family

to have a chip on one's shoulder — *être aigri*

when the chips are down — *dans les moments cruciaux*

Christmas: *Noël m*

happy Christmas; merry — *joyeux Noël*
Christmas

chuckle: *gloussement m, petit rire m*

chuckle; stifled laugh — *rire étouffé*

circumstance: *circonstance f*

under no circumstances; on no — *sous aucun prétexte; en*
account — *aucun cas*

clear: *clair,-e adj, évident,-e adj, net, nette adj*

I want to be clear in my own — *je veux en avoir le cœur net*
mind about it; I want to get to
the bottom of it

it's absolutely clear! — *c'est net et sans bavure!*

it is as clear as day; it's staring — *cela vous crève les yeux*
you in the face

to be a clear thinker — *avoir un esprit clair*

clear up: *éclaircir v*

can you throw any light on this — *pouvez-vous éclaircir cette*
question? — *question?*

to clear up an affair — *tirer une affaire au clair*

close: *fermer v*

I closed the door in his face — *je lui ai fermé la porte au nez*

close: *près adv, proche adj*

it was a close call — *on a eu chaud*

it was a close shave; it was a — *il était moins une (ou cinq)!*
near thing

close-mouthed: *taciturne adj*

mum's the word!; don't breathe a word!; close-lipped   *bouche consue!*

closure: *relâche m,f*

the theatre is closed   *le théâtre fait relâche*

clothes: *vêtements mpl, habits mpl*

she wears her clothes well   *elle porte bien la toilette*

clown: *guignol m*

to play the fool; to clown about; to act the clown   *faire le guignol*

coincidence: *coïncidence f*

by a curious coincidence (or chance)   *par un curieux hasard*

cold: *froid,-e adj; froid m*

it's bitterly cold   *il fait un froid de canard*

to be cool towards someone; to coldshoulder someone   *battre froid à quelqu'un*

come: *arriver v, venir v*

I'll call for you at seven o'clock   *je viendrai vous chercher à sept heures*

thank you for coming   *merci d'être venue*

to come/go to the help of   *venir/aller à l'aide de*

to come to the point   *en venir au fait*

to come to this   *en arriver là*

come back: *repasser v, revenir v*

I'll call in again; I'll come back   *je repasserai*

come down: *descendre v*

to come down off one's high horse   *descendre d'un cran*

come off: *se réaliser v*

to come off best (in a situation); to show oneself in a good light; to have the limelight   *avoir le beau rôle*

to come off well; to get off lightly   *s'en bien tirer*

come to pass: *advenir v*

come what may   *advienne que pourra*

comfort: *aise f, confort m*

to make oneself comfortable; to make oneself at home   *se mettre à son aise*

    company: compagnie *f*
to keep someone company   *tenir quelqu'un compagnie*
    compared to: à côté de *prep*
their car is large compared to   *leur voiture est grande à côté*
ours   *de la notre*
    compared with: auprès de *prep*
my pay is high compared with   *mon salaire est élevé auprès*
theirs   *du leur*
    comparison: comparaison *f*
there's no comparison!   *c'est le jour et la nuit!*
with regard to; in comparison   *par rapport à*
with; in relation to
    compose: composer *v*
composed (mainly) of; based   *à base de*
    conceited: avantageux,-euse *adj*
he is a conceited man; he is a   *il est un homme avantageux*
presuming fellow
    concern: concerner *v*
as far as I am concerned   *en ce qui me concerne*
    concession: concession *f*
to make concessions   *lâcher du lot*
    conclusion: conclusion *f*
it's a foregone conclusion   *c'est tout vu*
    condition: état *m*
in good condition   *en bon état*
    congratulations: compliments *mpl*, félicitations *fpl*
congratulations!   *mes compliments!; toutes*
    mes félicitations!

    connection: rapport *m*
what is it about?; what is it in   *c'est à quel propos?*
connection with?
    conscience: conscience *f*
deep within one's conscience;   *dans son for intérieur*
in one's heart of hearts
with a clear conscience   *en toute sûreté de conscience*
    consciousness: connaissance *f*
to lose/regain consciousness   *perdre/reprendre*
    connaissance

consequence: *conséquence f*
that is of no consequence — *cela ne tire pas à conséquence*

consider: *considérer v*
all things considered; on the whole — *toute réflexion faite; tout bien considéré*

consideration: *égard m*
out of consideration for — *par égard pour*

conspicuous: *bien en évidence f*
to be conspicuous by one's absence — *briller par son absence*

contrary: *contraire m*
on the contrary; on the other hand — *par contre*

convalescent: *convalescent adj*
to become convalescent — *entrer en convalescence*

cool: *sang-froid m*
to keep calm; to keep one's cool — *garder son sang-froid*

corner: *coin m, coincer v*
he got me out of a tight corner — *il m'a sauvé la mise*
it's not just round the corner; it won't happen in a hurry — *ce n'est pas pour demain*
to corner someone; to drive someone into a corner — *mettre quelqu'un au pied du mur*

correspondence: *courrier m, correspondance f*
he is dealing with his correspondence — *il fait son courrier*

cost: *coûter v*
at all costs; cost what it may — *coûte que coûte*
to cost an arm and a leg; to cost the earth — *coûter les yeux de la tête*

course: *cours m*
in due course; at the proper time — *en temps et lieu; en son temps*
in the course of the day; during the day — *au cours de la journée*

course (of): *naturellement adv*
of course — *bien entendu; bien sûr; bien évidemment*

court: *faire v la cour*

he is courting Denise — *il fait la cour à Denise*

cracking (to get): *s'y mettre v, se mettre v au boulot*

to get cracking; to get stuck in — *mettre les bouchées doubles*

crazy: *toqué,-e adj*

to be crazy (or mad) about someone* — *être toqué de quelqu'un ***

crestfallen: *déçu adj*

to look crestfallen; to have one's tail between one's legs — *avoir l'oreille basse*

cropper (to come a): *se planter v*

to come a cropper; to fall flat on one's face — *ramasser (ou prendre) une veste*

to come unstuck; to come a cropper; to find nobody in — *se casser le nez*

cross (oneself): *se signer v*

cross my heart and hope to die — *croix de bois, croix de fer si je mens je vais en enfer*

cross: *croiser v*

keep your fingers crossed for me — *fais une petite prière pour moi*

to cross one's fingers — *croiser les doigts*

to cross swords with someone — *se frotter à quelqu'un*

crowd: *foule f*

in the thick of the crowd/fray — *au plus fort de la foule/mêlée*

cruise: *croisière f*

to go on a cruise — *partir en croisière*

cry: *pleurer v*

to cry one's eyes out — *pleurer comme un veau (ou une madeleine)*

custom: *usage m, mœurs fpl*

customs (or manners) change with the times — *autres temps, autres mœurs*

it is customary to — *il est d'usage de (+inf)*

it's the custom; it's the way things are done — *c'est l'usage; c'est entré dans les mœurs*

cut: *couper v*

to cut the ground from under someone — *couper l'herbe sous les pieds à quelqu'un*

to cut to the quick — *blesser au vif*

D

damn: *éreinter v, damner v*

to damn someone with faint praise	*assommer quelqu'un avec des fleurs*
to damn with faint praise	*éreinter sous couleur d'éloge*

dance: *danse f*

he has led me a fine dance — *il m'en a fait de bleues*

darkness: *nuit f, obscurité f, ténèbres fpl*

it is getting (or growing) dark — *il se fait nuit*

the light is failing; darkness is approaching — *le jour baisse*

under cover of darkness — *à la faveur de la nuit*

date: *date f*

dated; dated from; under date of — *en date de*

to bring up to date — *mettre à jour*

what day of the month is it?; what date is it? — *à quel quantième sommes-nous?*

dawn: *aube f*

at dawn; at first light; at daybreak — *à l'aube; dès l'aube*

day: *jour m*

at daybreak; at the crack of dawn — *au point du jour; à l'aube*

every day — *tous les jours*

every other day; every two days — *tous les deux jours*

at the crack of dawn

139

delay

the day-to-day work is interesting	le travail de tous les jours est intéressant
to travel by day/by night	voyager de jour/de nuit
daylight: jour m	
it is beginning to get light	il commence à faire jour
it is broad daylight	il fait grand jour
dead: mort,-e adj	
more dead than alive; frightened to death	plus mort que vif
deaf: sourd,-e adj	
deaf-mute; deaf-and-dumb person	sourd-muet; sourde-muette
he is stone deaf; he's as deaf as a post	il est sourd comme un pot
to turn a deaf ear to	faire la sourde oreille à
deal: marché m	
it's a deal	marché conclu
it's in the bag; the deal is all sewn up	l'affaire est dans le sac
death: mort f	
to be at death's door	être à l'article de la mort
to be within an ace of death; to be at death's door	être à deux doigts de la mort
to starve to death; to die of hunger	mourir de faim
debt: dette f	
he has got into debt; he has run up debts	il a fait des dettes
he is crippled with debts; he is up to his ears in debt	il est criblé de dettes
deceased: feu,-e adj	
my late father	feu mon père; mon feu père
decision: décision f	
to make a decision on the spot	prendre une décision séance tenante
definitely: absolument adv, bien sûr adv, vraiment adv	
do you think so? yes definitely	vous trouvez? oui, vraiment
without fail; definitely	à coup sûr
delay: tarder v	
without delay	sans tarder

delight: *prendre v plaisir, enchanter v, ravir v*

I am delighted to see you	*je suis ravi de vous voir*
to be delighted; to be in the seventh heaven	*être aux anges*
very pleased to meet you; delighted to meet you	*enchanté/ravi de vous connaître*

delirious (be): *délirer v*

to be delirious	*battre la campagne*

demoralize: *abattre v*

don't let things get you down (or demoralize you)	*ne te laisse pas abattre*

depth: *profondeur f*

to be out of one's depth; to lose one's footing	*perdre pied*

design: *dessein m, intention f*

to have designs on	*avoir des vues sur*

desire: *envie f, désir m*

I have a desire to	*j'ai envie de*

despair: *désespoir m*

he is in despair	*il est au désespoir*
in desperation; as a last resource	*en désespoir de cause*

devil: *diable m*

there is no holding him; he has the devil in him	*il a le diable au corps*
to go to the dogs; to go to the devil	*s'en aller à tous les diables*

die: *mourir v*

to die a natural death	*mourir de sa belle mort*
to die of grief; to die of a broken heart	*mourir de chagrin*

diet: *régime m, diète f*

slimming diet	*régime amaigrissant*
to be on a diet	*être au régime; suivre un régime*

differently: *autrement adv*

we'll have to go about it quite differently	*il faut s'y prendre tout autrement*

difficult: *difficile adj*

it is not so very difficult	*ce n'est pas la mer à boire*

difficulty: difficulté f, peine f

to get out of a difficulty; to get out of trouble	*se tirer d'affaire*
to hit a snag; to run into a difficulty; to be stymied	*tomber sur un bec*
with/without difficulty	*avec/sans peine*

disease: maladie f

this disease is catching — *cette maladie s'attrape facilement*

disinclined: peu disposé adj, peu enclin adj

unwilling to do; disinclined to do — *être peu disposé à faire*

dislocate: démettre v

he dislocated his wrist — *il s'est démis le poignet*

dismount: descendre v de

to dismount (from a horse) — *descendre de cheval*

disregard: mépris m

he has no regard for conventions — *il n'a pas le mépris des convenances*

distance: distance f, loin m, lointain m, trotte f

in the distance — *au loin; dans le loin; au lointain; dans le lointain*

it's quite a way from here; it's a fair distance from here — *ça fait une trotte*

distinguish: distinguer v

I cannot distinguish between them — *je n'arrive pas à trouver de différence entre eux*

disturb: déranger v

I trust that I am not disturbing you? — *je ne vous dérange pas?*

dive: piquer v un plongeon

he took a header into the pool; he dived headfirst into the pool — *il a piqué une tête dans la piscine*

do: faire v

he does as he pleases; he goes his own way	*il en fait à sa tête*
he does it all without trying	*il fait tout cela en se jouant*
I do a lot of driving	*je fais beaucoup de voiture*
I wouldn't do that for anything in the world	*je ne ferais cela pour rien au monde*
no sooner said than done	*aussitôt dit, aussitôt fait*

to take hours doing something	*mettre des heures à faire qelque chose*
what are you doing tonight?	*qu'est-ce que tu fais ce soir?*
what job do you do?; what is your line of business?	*quel métier faites-vous?*

faisiez did your do?

dog (follow): *suivre v*

to dog the steps of; to follow closely	*s'attacher aux pas de*

doubt: *doute m*

doubtless; no doubt; probably	*sans doute*
there is no doubt that	*il est hors de doute que; il ne fait aucune doute que*
without any doubt	*sans nul doute*

doubt: *douter v*

there is no doubt about it	*il n'y a pas à s'y tromper*
there's no doubt about it; there's no denying it	*il n'y a pas à dire*

downstairs: *en bas m*

he lives downstairs/upstairs	*il habite en bas/en haut*

downstream: *en aval m*

the lock is downstream	*l'écluse est en aval d'ici*

draw (sport): *match m nul, partie f nulle,*

the match ended in a draw	*ils ont fini par faire match nul (ou partie nulle)*

draw: *tirer v*

to draw lots	*tirer au sort*
to draw to a close; to run low	*tirer à sa fin*

drench: *mouiller v, tremper v*

drenched to the skin	*mouillé/trempé jusqu'aux os*

dress: *habillement m, vêtements mpl, tenue f*

a general (or all) purpose outfit (clothes)	*une tenue passe-partout*
in evening dress	*en tenue soirée*
in full dress; in full uniform	*en grande tenue*
to be particular in one's dress; to take pride in one's appearance	*soigner sa mise*

dress: *habiller v*

he is well dressed	*il est bien mis*
she is washing and dressing; she is getting ready	*elle fait sa toilette*

to be dressed up to the nines; to be dressed to kill	*être tiré à quatre épingles*
to get dressed up; to get spruced up	*se faire beau; se faire belle*

dressing down (give): *passer v un savon à*

I got a good ticking off/dressing down	*j'ai reçu un bon savon*

drink: *boire v*

to drink at the bar	*boire sur le zinc*
to drink by oneself; to be a solitary drinker	*boire en Suisse*
to drink greedily; to gulp down	*boire à grandes gorgées*
to drink like a fish	*boire à tire-larigot*
to have a drink	*boire un coup; boire un verre*

je voudrais boire une verre *(handwritten)*

drink: *boisson f*

to have had one too many; to be tipsy	*avoir un verre dans le nez*

drink to: *arroser v*

that calls for a drink!	*cela s'arrose!*

drive: *pousser v*

he exhausted my patience; he drove me to the limit	*il a me poussé à bout*
to drive all night	*rouler toute la nuit*
to drive into a corner	*pousser dans ses derniers retranchements*

drop a hint: *faire v une allusion*

to have a word with someone; to drop a hint to someone	*toucher un mot à quelqu'un*

drop off (set down): *déposer v*

to drop someone off at the corner	*déposer quelqu'un au coin de la rue*

due to: *dû, due adj à, attribuable adj à*

on account of; due to; because of	*en raison de*

dumbfound: *ahurir v, sidérer* v*

to be dumbfounded	*en rester baba*

dump: *larguer v, se débarasser v de*

to dump; to ditch; to pack in; to leave in the lurch	*planter là*

dumps (spirits): le cafard

to be down in the dumps	avoir le moral à zéro
to be right down in the dumps; to be at a very low ebb	être dans le trente-sixième dessous

during: pendant *prep*

during this time; meanwhile — pendant ce temps

dusk: crépuscule *m*

at dusk; in the twilight — entre chien et loup

duty: devoir *m*, fonction *f*

to commence one's duties; to take office	entrer en fonctions
to make it one's duty to do	se faire un devoir de faire

reached here
13/1/02

E

nous sommes arrivé
quelques minutes
plus tôt/tard

earlier: auparavant *adv*, plus tôt *adv*

an hour earlier	une heure plus tôt
to leave earlier	partir de meilleure heure
two months before; two months earlier	deux mois auparavant

earliest: le plus tôt *adv*

at your earliest convenience — aussitôt que vous le pourrez

possible

early, soon: tôt *adj & adv*, de bonne heure *adj*

as soon as possible; as early as possible	le plus tôt possible
at the earliest	au plus tôt
very early	de très bonne heure

earn: gagner *v*

to earn one's crust; to earn one's bread and butter	gagner sa croûte; gagner son bifteck
to earn one's keep	gagner de quoi vivre
to earn one's living	gagner sa vie; gagner son pain

ease: aise *f*

to be (or feel) ill at ease; to be uneasy	être mal à l'aise (ou peu à l'aise)
to be (or feel) at ease; to be comfortable; to be well-off	être à son aise; être à l'aise

easy: *facile adj*

it's as easy as can be	*c'est facile comme tout*
it's as easy as pie; it's dead simple	*c'est bête comme chou*
it's dead easy	*c'est simple comme bonjour (ou chou)*
no easy task; it's not easy to see	*ce n'est pas évident*
there's really nothing to it; it's easy	*ce n'est pas bien sorcier*

economy: *économie f*

for the sake of economy	*par économie*

edge (one's way): *se faufiler v*

to steal to the door; to edge one's way to the door	*se faufiler vers la porte*

effect: *effet m*

to have an effect on someone	*faire quelque chose à quelqu'un*

effort: *effort m*

he has made every effort to	*il a fait tous ses efforts pour*
to make a big effort; to work really hard	*en mettre un coup*

egg: *œuf m*

it's like the curate's egg — good in parts	*il y a à prendre et à laisser*

elbow: *coude m*

to elbow one's way	*jouer des coudes; avancer en jouant des coudes*

end: *bout m, but m, fin m*

at the end of the day; when all is said and done	*en fin de compte*
to be at the end of one's tether	*être au bout (de son rouleau)*
to be at the end of one's tether; to be at one's wits' end	*être au bout de son latin*
to draw to an end	*toucher (ou tirer) à sa fin*
to put an end to	*mettre fin à*
we'll never see the end of this	*on n'en verra jamais la fin*

enjoy: *aimer v, jouir v de, trouver v plaisir à, se plaire v*

did you enjoy the concert?	*le concert vous a-t-il plu?*

he enjoys good health	*il jouit d'une bonne santé*
I really enjoy music	*je trouve beaucoup de plaisir à la musique*
she enjoys being in Venice	*elle se plaît à Venise*
enjoy (oneself): *s'amuser v*	*vous vous êtes*
did you enjoy yourself in Nice?	*est-ce que tu t'es bien amusé à Nice?*

enough: *assez adj & adv*	
enough said, let's have some action!	*assez parlé, des actes!*
I've had enough!; enough is enough!	*c'est assez!; c'en est assez!; en voilà assez!*
that's enough thank you	*cela suffit, merci; c'est assez, merci*
we have enough and to spare	*nous en avons à revendre*
envious: *envieux,-euse adj*	
to cast envious eyes upon	*regarder d'un œil d'envie*
envy: *envie f, jalousie f*	
to be green with envy	*être vert de jalousie*
to make someone green with envy	*faire pâlir (ou loucher) quelqu'un de jalousie*
equal: *égal,-e adj*	
he is not equal to it	*il n'est pas à la hauteur*
on an equal footing; as equals	*sur le même pied; sur un pied d'égalité*
other things being equal	*toutes choses égales*
especially: *spécialement adv*	
especially as; since	*surtout que*
even: *même adv*	
even though; even if	*quand bien même*
event: *événement m*	
at all events; at any rate; anyway	*en tout cas*
ever: *jamais adv*	
if ever you pass through Paris, come and see me	*si jamais tu passes par Paris, viens moi voir*
for ever (and ever)	*à tout jamais; pour jamais*
every: *tout,-e adj*	
every day I go out shopping	*tous les jours je sors faire des courses*

extent

everywhere: *partout adv*
everywhere that; wherever　　　*partout où*
exactly: *exactement adv, précisément adv*
I don't know exactly　　　*je ne sais pas trop*
example: *exemple m*
for example; for instance　　　*par exemple*
excuse: *excuser v*
if you'll excuse the expression　　　*passer-moi l'expression*
to excuse; to spare someone　　　*faire grâce à quelqu'un de*
　　　　quelque chose
exhaust: *épuiser v*
to be flustered; to be exhausted;　*battre de l'aile*
to be on one's last legs
expect: *attendre v, s'attendre v à, vouloir v*
to be expecting a baby　　　*attendre un bébé; attendre un*
　　　　enfant
to expect something　　　*s'attendre à quelque chose*
what can you expect?　　　*que voulez-vous?*
what do you expect me to do　　　*que voulez-vous que j'y*
about it?　　　*fasse?*
expectation: *attente f, prévision f*
against all expectations　　　*contre toute apparence*
quite unexpectedly; contrary to　*contre toute attente*
expectation
expense: *dépense f, frais m*
I have met my expenses　　　*j'ai fait face à mes dépenses*
to cover one's expenses　　　*faire ses frais*
experienced: *versé,-e adj*　Nous êtes
he is very experienced in these　*il est très versé dans ces*
matters　　　*matières*
expert: *spécialiste m,f, connaisseur m, expert m*
he is an expert judge of wines　*il se connait parfaitement en*
　　　　vins
explanation: *explication(s) f, fpl*
I demand an explanation　　　*j'exige des explications*
extent: *mesure f, degré m*
to a certain extent; to some　*dans une certaine mesure*
extent

extreme: *extrême adj*

to go from one extreme to another	*tomber d'un excès dans un autre; aller (ou passer) du blanc au noir*

eye: *œil m, yeux mpl*

in a trice; in the twinkling of an eye	*en un clin d'œil*
to be very much in the public eye	*être très en vue*
to have a good eye; to have good judgement	*avoir le compas dans l'œil*
to keep a close eye on someone	*surveiller quelqu'un de près*
to keep one's eyes open	*ne pas avoir les yeux dans sa poche*
to make eyes at someone	*lancer des œillades à quelqu'un*
to see eye to eye with	*entrer dans les vues de*

eyewash: *collyre m (med)*

that's a lot of eyewash; that's all window dressing	*c'est de la frime*

F

face: *faire v face à*

to face the music	*tenir tête à l'orage; braver l'orage*
to look out on to; to face; to give access to	*donner sur*

face: *visage m, mine f*

to have (or to pull) a long face	*avoir la mine longue (ou allongée)*
to put on a bold (or brave) face	*faire bonne contenance*

fact: *fait m*

as a matter of fact; in point of fact; in fact	*en fait; de fait; par le fait*
the fact is that; as a matter of fact	*le fait est que*
the fact remains that	*toujours est-il que*

to have the facts at one's fingertips	connaître les faits sur le bout du doigt

fail: échouer *v*, être *v* collé

to fail (an examination)	être refusé (à un examen)
without fail	sans faute; à coup sûr

faint: s'évanouir *v*

to feel faint with hunger	tomber d'inanition

fall: chute *f*

to have a fall	faire une chute

fall: tomber *v*

the rain is falling heavily	la pluie tombe dru
to fall backwards	tomber à la renverse
to fall full length	tomber de tout son long
to jump out of the frying-pan into the fire	tomber de Charybde en Scylla

far: loin *adv*

as far back as I remember	du plus loin que je me souviens
by a long way; by far; far and away	de beaucoup
far from it	à beaucoup près
far from it!; not by a long way!	tant s'en faut!; loin de là!
how far?	jusqu'où?
I'm not displeased, far from it	je ne suis pas mécontent, bien loin de là
to; as far as; right up to; all the way to	jusqu'à la; jusqu'au

farthing: liard *m*

not to have a brass farthing	ne pas avoir un rouge liard

fashion: façon *f*

as well as possible; after a fashion; so-so	tant bien que mal

fashion: mode *f*, vogue *f*

out of date; out of fashion	passé de mode
to be in circulation; to be fashionable	être de mise
to be in fashion; to be fashionable	en vogue

fast (be): *avancer v*

your watch is five minutes fast   *votre montre avance de cinq*
    minutes

fault: *défaut m*

to find fault with something   *trouver à redire à quelque*
    chose

favour: *faveur f*

to be in favour of doing   *être d'avis de faire quelque*
something   *chose*

feather (fatten): *engraisser v*

to feather one's nest; to make   *faire sa pelote*
one's pile

to feather one's nest   *mettre du foin dans ses*
    bottes

fed up (be): *en avoir v assez, en avoir v marre*

to be fed up; to be cheesed off   *en avoir assez; en avoir marre*

to have had it up to here; to be   *en avoir plein les bottes;*
fed up to the back teeth   *en avoir par-dessus la tête;*
    en avoir plein le dos

feed: *manger v*

to give someone food (or   *donner à manger à quelqu'un*
something to eat)

feel: *se sentir v, se trouver v*

I feel quite (or very) comfortable   *je me trouve très bien ici*
here

I work when I feel like it   *je travaille quand ça me plaît*

not to feel up to it; to feel off   *ne pas se sentir d'attaque*
form

to be feeling great   *avoir le moral*

to feel a bit off form   *se sentir un peu chose*

to feel off-colour; to feel a bit   *se sentir patraque*
under the weather

fellow: *type m, gaillard m, zig ou zigue m*

a nice bloke*; a decent fellow   *bon zigue*; bon zig**

strapping fellow   *gaillard bien bâti*

fettle (fine): *en pleine forme f*

to be in fine fettle; to be in   *avoir la pêche*
top form

151

fiddle: *carotter v*

he is always trying to fiddle a bit for himself — *il essaie toujours de carotter*

she fiddles the housekeeping money — *elle carotte sur l'argent des commissions*

figure: *chiffre m*

in plain figures — *en chiffres connus*

figure: *ligne f*

to have a slim figure — *avoir la ligne*

final: *dernier,-ière adj*

after all; in the final analysis — *au bout du compte*

financial difficulty: *gêne f*

he is in great financial difficulties — *il est dans une grande gêne*

find: *trouvaille f*

I've made a find at the antique shop — *j'ai fait une trouvaille au magasin d'antiquités*

find: *trouver v, découvrir v*

he has found out what is going on; he has got to the the bottom of things — *il a découvert le pot aux roses*

to come up with a solution; to find a way — *trouver le joint*

fine: *bien adv*

everything is fine!; really super-duper! — *ça baigne!; tout baigne!*

that's fine! — *à la bonne heure!*

finish: *achever v, finir v, terminer v*

I have finished shaving — *j'ai achevé de me raser*

to be a close finish — *finir dans un mouchoir*

fire: *feu m*

he's no bright spark; he will never set the Thames on fire — *il n'a pas inventé la poudre*

he set the house on fire — *il a mis le feu à la maison*

the house has caught fire — *la maison a pris feu*

the house is on fire — *la maison est en feu*

first (at): *abord m (d')*

at first he didn't know anyone — *d'abord il ne connaissait personne* — *je ne connaissais*

from the very first — *dès le premier abord*

first-rate: excellent,-e adj, de premier ordre adj

first-rate	*de première force; de premier ordre*

fish: poisson m

here's a pretty kettle of fish!	*en voila une affaire!*
I have other fish to fry; I have more important things to do	*j'ai autre chats à fouetter*
that's a different kettle of fish; that's another story	*c'est une autre paire de manches*

fit (to see): trouver v bon, juger v bon

if you see fit	*si bon vous semble*

fix: pétrin m

to be in a fix (or fine mess)	*être dans de beaux draps*

flabbergast: sidérer v, époustoufler v

I was flabbergasted	*j'en suis resté bleu*

flame (old): ancien(ne) m,f

to meet by chance an old flame	*rencontrer un(e) ancien(ne)*

flash: éclair m

to go off like a flash (or greased lightning)	*partir comme un éclair*

flawless: parfait adj

flawless; faultless	*sans bavure*

flea: puce f

to put a flea in someone's ear	*mettre la puce à l'oreille à quelqu'un*
to send someone off with a flea in their ear	*envoyer promener quelqu'un**

here's a pretty kettle of fish

flesh: *chair f*

in the flesh; as large as life	*en chair et en os*
it makes my flesh creep; it gives me goose pimples	*j'en ai la chair de poule*
to be neither flesh, fowl nor good red herring	*ce n'est ni chair ni poisson*

float: *flotter v*

to float on one's back	*faire la planche*

flood: *inonder v*

flooded with light	*inondé de lumière, inondé de clarté*

fly: *voler v*

as the crow flies	*à vol d'oiseau*
to fly to pieces; to be shattered	*voler en éclats*

fly off (the handle): *s'emporter v, sortir v de ses gonds*

to get huffy; to fly off the handle	*prendre la mouche*

foil: *contrecarrer v*

to foil someone; to thwart somebody's plans	*faire échec à quelqu'un*

follow: *suivre v*

follow me	*suivez-moi*
to follow suit; to do the same	*en faire autant*

following: *suite f*

as the result of	*à la suite de*

fool (= deceive): *tromper v*

that doesn't fool anybody	*cela ne trompe personne*

fool: *faire v l'imbécile, faire v l'idiote*

down-right ass; absolute fool	*sot achevé*
he is a downright fool (or ass)	*il est bête à manger du foin*
I felt such a fool	*je me suis vraiment senti bête*
to make a fool of oneself; to make oneself look ridiculous	*se rendre ridicule aux yeux de tous*
to make an April fool of	*donner un poisson d'avril à*
to play the fool	*faire des bêtises*
to play the fool; to act the goat	*faire le loustic*
to play the fool	*faire le zouave*

foot: *pied m*

to be flat-footed	*avoir les pieds plats*

to foot it; to hoof it; to go on foot	*aller à pinces**
to put one's foot in it	*mettre les pieds dans le plat*
forbid: interdire v	
it is forbidden to smoke; smoking prohibited	*il est interdit de fumer*
force (in): en vigueur f	
the regulation is now in force	*le règlement est actuellement en vigueur*
force: force f	
by force of circumstances	*par la force des choses*
fork out: se fendre v	
to fork out for something	*se fendre de quelque chose*
form: forme f, condition f	
he is in good form; he is in good spirits	*il est en train d'attaque*
on form; in top form	*d'attaque*
he's on top form today	*il est remonté à bloc aujourd'hui*
to do something as a matter of form (or for form's sake)	*faire quelque chose par manière d'acquit*
fortnight: quinzaine f	
for a fortnight	*pour quinze jours; pour une quinzaine*
fortunately: heureusement adv	
fortunately; luckily	*par bonheur*
foursome: à quatre	
a foursome (two men, two women); a wife-swapping party	*une partie carrée*
freckle: tache f de rousseur	
freckled	*piqueté de taches de rousseur*
freeze: geler v	
i's freezing hard	*il gèle à pierre fendre*
friend: ami m, amie f, copain m, copine f	
they're as thick as thieves	*ils sont amis (ou copains) comme cochons**
friendship: amitié f	
a short (or short-lived) friendship	*une amitié de courte durée*
to befriend someone; to take a liking to someone	*prendre quelqu'un en amitié*

to make friends with someone	*se lier d'amitié avec quelqu'un*
frighten: *effrayer* v, *faire* v *peur à*	
he was more frightened than hurt	*il a eu plus de peur que de mal*
fritter: *gaspiller* v, *perdre* v	
to fritter away one's money	*dépenser tout son argent en bêtises*
frog: *grenouille* f	
to have a frog in one's throat	*avoir un chat dans la gorge*
frown: *froncer* v *les sourcils, se renfrogner* v	
to frown; to knit one's brows	*froncer les sourcils*
full: *plein,-e* adj	
chock-full; full to bursting	*plein comme un œuf*
full swing: *libre cours* m	
to be at its height; to be in full swing	*battre son plein*
fun (have): *s'amuser* v	
to have fun doing; to enjoy oneself doing	*s'amuser à faire*
we had a great time; we had great fun	*nous nous sommes bien amusés*
fundamental: *fondemental,-e* adj	
fundamental question	*question de fond*
funny: *drôle* adj, *amusant* adj	
it was terribly funny	*c'était amusant comme tout*
further: *plus loin* adv	
I would go even further	*j'irais même plus loin*
fuss: *façons* fpl, *des histoires* fpl	
he is making a fuss	*il fait ses façons*
there's nothing to make a fuss about	*il n'y a pas de quoi fouetter un chat*
to kick up a fuss; to kick up a shindy	*faire du foin*
to make a fuss about (or over); to make a great deal of fuss	*faire un tas d'histoires*
future: *avenir* m	
an up-and-coming man; a man with a future	*un homme d'avenir*
in future; from now on	*à l'avenir*

to make provision for someone's *assurer l'avenir de quelqu'un*
future

G

gab: *bagou(t)* m
he has the gift of the gab | *il a la langue bien pendue; il a*
du bagou

gaffe: *gaffe* f
to make a gaffe; to drop a brick; *faire une gaffe*
to drop a clanger
gain: *gagner* v
to gain ground | *gagner du terrain*
game: *jeu* m
to beat someone at his own | *battre quelqu'un à son*
game | *propre jeu*
gape: *rester* v *bouche bée*
I stood gaping with | *je suis resté bouche bée*
astonishment | *d'étonnement*
generally: *généralement* adv, *en général* adv
generally speaking; as a general | *d'une manière générale*
rule
genius: *génie* m
he bears the stamp of genius | *il est marqué au coin de génie*
get even: *se venger* v
to get one's own back on | *rattraper quelqu'un au*
somebody | *tournant*
get off: *s'en tirer* v
to get off lightly; to be well out | *en être quitte à bon compte*
of it
get on: *s'entendre* v
to get on well/badly together | *faire bon/mauvais ménage*
we get on well together | *nous nous entendons très*
bien

get out: *descendre* v
to get out of the car/the train | *descendre de voiture/du train*
get out: *tirer* v
to get out while the going is | *tirer son épingle du jeu*
good; to play one's game well

157

gift: *don m, talent m*

to have a flair for something; to have a gift for something — *avoir la bosse de quelque chose*

giggle: *petit rire m sot, rire m bébête*

he did it for a giggle — *il a fait ça pour rigoler*

giggle: *avoir v le fou rire*

to giggle — *avoir le fou rire*

give: *donner v*

to give rise to — *donner lieu à; donner sujet de*

give up: *abandonner v*

to give something up as lost — *faire son deuil de quelque chose*

give way: *céder v*

to give way; to give ground; to retreat — *lâcher pied*

glance: *regard m, coup m d'œil*

he glanced in my direction — *il a jeté un coup d'œil vers moi*

to steal a glance at someone; to give someone a surreptitious glance — *regarder quelqu'un à la dérobée*

glare: *lancer v un regard furieux*

to glare at one another — *se regarder en chiens de faïence*

go: *aller v, passer v, marcher v*

everything was going splendidly — *tout marche à souhait*

it goes without saying; it's self-evident — *cela va de soi*

to go at a furious rate — *aller à un train d'enfer*

to go along at one's own pace — *aller son (petit) train*

to go down the street — *passer dans la rue*

to go from bad to worse — *aller de mal en pis*

to go on all fours; on one's hands and knees — *marcher à quatre pattes*

to go to pot; to go to the dogs — *aller à la dérive*

go-ahead: *feu m vert*

to give someone the green light; to give the go-ahead — *donner le feu vert à quelqu'un*

go away: s'en aller *v*

go away, you're disturbing me!   *allez-vous en, vous me dérangez!*

go beyond: dépasser *v*

it's above me; that's beyond me   *c'est trop fort pour moi*

goat: bouc *m*, chèvre *f*

to be the scapegoat   *être le bouc émissaire*

godsend: aubaine *f*

to be a godsend; to be heaven sent   *tomber du ciel*

gold: or *m*

it's a rock-solid investment; it's a gold mine   *c'est de l'or en barre*

good-looker: beau garcon *m*; belle femme *f*

he's a good looker   *il est beau gosse; c'est un beau gars*

she's a good looker   *c'est un beau brin de fille; c'est une jolie fille*

good: bien *adj*

to be on good terms with someone   *être bien avec quelqu'un*

good: bon *m*, bien *m*,

a fat lot of good that will do him*   *ça lui fera une belle jambe*

a good man; a wealthy man; a man of property   *un homme de bien*

good people; well-to-do people   *des gens de bien*

he's gone for good   *il est parti pour tout de bon*

what good does that do me?   *à quoi cela m'avance-t-il?*

what good is it to (+vb); what would be the point of (+vb)   *à quoi sert de (+inf)*

goodbye: adieu *m*

to say goodbye to someone   *faire ses adieux à quelqu'un*

goose: oie *f*, poule *f*

he cannot say boo to a goose   *c'est une poule mouillée*

gossip: bavarder *v*, papoter *v*

they gossip; they natter   *elles taillent des bavettes*

go to see: aller *v* trouver

go and see the boss about this question   *allez trouver le patron pour cette question*

gradually: *graduellement adv*

little by little; gradually · · · · · · · · · · *petit à petit; peu à peu*

greenhorn: *jeunot m*

to be a greenhorn; to be a · · · · · · · · *être un bleu*
beginner

grind: *grincer v (dents)*

to grind one's teeth; to gnash · · · · · · *grincer des dents*
one's teeth

grudge: *rancune f*

he bears me a grudge · · · · · · · · · · · · *il me garde rancune*

guard: *garde f*

to be on one's guard; to watch · · · · · · *être (ou se tenir) sur ses*
out · *gardes*

guard: *garder v*

to be on one's guard; to be · · · · · · · · *se tenir sur la réserve*
reserved about

guesswork: *conjecture f, hypothèse f*

by guesswork · · · · · · · · · · · · · · · · · · · *au jugé*

H

hair: *cheveux mpl*

her hair was dishevelled · · · · · · · · · · *elle a les cheveux en bataille*

hale: *vigoreux,-euse adj, robuste adj*

hale and hearty · · · · · · · · · · · · · · · · · *frais et gaillard*

half: *moitié f*

we halved the cake between us; · · · · · · *on a partagé le gateau moitié*
we shared the cake half and half

halve: *partager v en deux*

to go halves with someone · · · · · · · · · *se mettre de moitié avec*
· *quelqu'un*

hand (cards): *jeu m*

to have all the right cards; to · · · · · · · *avoir beau jeu; avoir du jeu*
have a good hand

to show one's hand; to lay · · · · · · · · · *abattre son jeu*
one's cards on the table

hand: *main f*

a helping hand · · · · · · · · · · · · · · · · · · *coup de main*

give me a hand!	*donne-moi un coup de main!*
hands off!	*à bas les mains!*
to have everything at hand	*avoir tout sous la main*
to shake hands with someone	*serrer la main de quelqu'un*

hangover: *gueule f de bois, mal m aux cheveux*

to have a hangover	*avoir une gueule de bois;*
	avoir mal aux cheveux

happen: *arriver v, se passer v*

it could happen to anyone	*cela peut arriver à n'importe qui*
it happened yesterday	*c'est arrivé hier*
it's bound to happen	*cela arrivera comme mars en carême*
it so happens that I was there; I happened to be there	*il se trouve que j'étais là*
what's the matter?; what's happening?; what's going on?	*que se passe-t-il?*

harass: *tracasser v*

to be tired; to be harassed; to be under pressure	*être sur les dents*

hard-up: *fauché,-e adj*

to live from hand to mouth; to be hard up	*tirer le diable par le queue*

hard: *dur,-e adj*

he is hard of hearing	*il a l'oreille dure*

harp: *rabâcher v*

to harp on the same old theme	*chanter toujours la même antienne*

have: *avoir v*

I've had it	*je suis fichu*
they've had it!; it's all over for us!	*les carottes sont cuites!*
to have it in for	*en avoir contre; avoir une dent contre*
to have what it takes	*avoir ce qu'il faut*

have just: *venir v de*

she had just got up	*elle venait de se lever*

head: *tête f*

from head to foot; from top to toe	*de pied en cap; de la tête aux pieds*

to fall head over heels	*faire la culbute*
heads or tails?	*à pile ou face?*
I can't make head nor tail of it	*j'y perds mon latin*
to stand on one's head	*se tenir sur sa tête*
to take it into one's head to	*se mettre dans la tête de*

head for: *se diriger v*

to head for port (ship)	*mettre le cap sur le port*

health: *santé f*

cheers!; good health!	*à votre santé!; santé!*
in bad/good health	*en mauvaise/bonne santé*
your very good health!; cheers!	*à la bonne vôtre!*
to drink someone's health	*boire à la santé de quelqu'un*

hear: *entendre v*

I have heard of him	*j'ai entendu parler de lui*
I have heard (that)	*j'ai entendu parler de;*
	j'ai entendu dire que
I've heard it all before	*je connais la chanson (ou la musique)*
unless one hears to the contrary	*sauf avis contraire*

heart: *cœur m*

to be open-handed; to be big hearted	*avoir le cœur sur la main*
to learn by heart	*apprendre par cœur*
to take something to heart	*prendre quelque chose à cœur*

heaven: *ciel m, paradis m, là-haut adv*

he is upstairs; he is in heaven	*il est là-haut*
he's in the seventh heaven; he's on cloud nine	*il est au septième ciel*

hell: *enfer m*

you can go to hell for all I care*	*tu peux crever la gueule ouverte*

help: *aide f, secours m*

not if I can help it!	*pas si bête*
to be a great help to	*être d'un grand secours à*

help: *aider v*

I can't help it	*c'est plus fort que moi*
it cannot be helped; there is nothing to be done	*il n'y a rien à faire*
that doesn't help anything	*cela n'arrange rien*

here: ici *adv*

here and there; in places	*de place en place; par places*
here and there; on this side and that	*deçà delà*
here and there; this way and that way	*çà et là*
the bus comes as far as here	*le bus vient jusqu'ici*

hesitation: *hésitation f*

without thinking twice about it; without a moments hesitation — *sans faire ni une ni deux*

hinder: *gêner v*

am I in your way?; am I hindering you? — *est-ce que je vous gêne?*

hindrance: *gêne f*

without let or hindrance; without mishap — *sans encombre*

hint: *allusion f, insinuation f*

to drop a hint — *faire une allusion*

hit: *succès m*

he'll be a great hit; he will be a sensation — *il va faire un malheur*

to be a smash hit; to be a roaring success (entertainment) — *faire un tabac*

hit: *frapper v, atteindre v*

to hit the bull's-eye; to hit the nail on the head — *mettre dans le mille; mettre dans le noir*

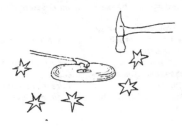

to be a smash hit

to hit the nail on the head; to strike home	*frapper juste*
hitch-hike: *faire v du stop*	
they hitch-hiked to Paris	*ils ont fait du stop jusqu'à Paris*
to thumb a lift; to hitch-hike	*voyager sur le pouce*
hold: *tenir v*	
he can hold his liquor (or drink)	*il peut supporter l'alcool (ou la boisson)*
they were holding hands	*ils se tenaient par la main*
to hold out; to stand fast; to hold one's ground	*tenir bon; tenir ferme*
to hold someone spellbound; to keep someone in suspense	*tenir en haleine*
holiday: *vacances fpl*	
to go (away) on holiday	*partir en vacances*
we are taking our holiday in France	*nous prenons nos vacances en France*
home: *chez-moi m, inv*	
on my return home; back home	*de retour chez moi*
homesickness: *nostalgie f*	
to feel homesick	*avoir la nostalgie de son pays*
hook: *accrocher v*	
to be hooked; to have the habit	*être accro*
hop: *sauter v*	
to hop (on one foot)	*sauter (ou aller) à cloche-pied*
hopeless: *lamentable adj, nul, nulle adj*	
hopeless; a disgrace; beneath contempt	*au dessous de tout*
hot (=clever): *calé,-e adj*	
he's pretty hot at football	*il est très calé en football*
house: *maison f*	
to keep open house	*tenir table ouverte*
housekeeping, housework: *ménage m*	
to do the housework	*faire le ménage*
to look after one's house; to keep house	*tenir le ménage*
how: *comment adv*	
how come?; how is it?	*comment ça se fait?*
how do you mean?	*comment donc?*

how is it that he has gone?	*comment se fait-il qu'il soit parti?*
however: *de quelque manière adv, quelque ... que adv*	
however he may do it	*de quelque manière qu'il le fasse*
however strong he may be	*quelque fort qu'il soit*
however that may be; be that as it may	*quoi qu'il en soit*
huff: *mouche f*	
to slam the door; to walk out in a huff	*(faire) claquer la porte*
hurry: *hâte f*	
I'm in a hurry	*je suis pressé*
he won't come back here again in a hurry!	*il ne reviendra pas de sitôt!*
there's no great hurry; there's no panic	*il n'y a pas le feu*
hurry away: *se sauver v*	
it's getting late, I must hurry off	*il se fait tard, je me sauve*

I

idea: *idée f*	
to have an idea that	*avoir dans l'idée que*
ill: *malade adj*	
to be taken ill	*tomber malade*
ill luck: *déveine f*	
to be out of luck; to have a losing streak	*avoir la déveine; être dans la déveine*
imagine: *(s') imaginer v, se figurer v*	
imagine the situation; picture the situation	*figurez-vous la situation*
you can imagine how angry I was!	*pensez si j'étais furieux!*
immediately: *immédiatement adv*	
immediately; at once	*tout de suite*
immediately; at once; straightaway	*sur-le-champ; sur l'heure*

    impress: impressioner v

it's just for show; it's just to impress   *c'est pour la frime*

    impression: effet m, impression f

that gives a good impression   *cela fait bon effet*

    improve: améliorer v

to improve on acquaintance   *gagner à être connu*

    inadvertently: par inadvertance adv

inadvertently; accidently; by mistake   *par mégarde*

    including: compris,-e adj

including; inclusive; included   *y compris; compris; inclus*

    income: rentes fpl, revenu m

to have a private income   *avoir des rentes*

to live on (or have) a private income   *vivre de ses rentes*

to live up to one's income; to live beyond one's income   *dépenser tout son revenu*

    inconsiderate type: sans-gêne m,f inv

he is offhand; he is an inconsiderate type   *il est un sans-gêne*

    indebted (be): être v obligé

to be outdone by someone; to be indebted to someone   *être (ou demeurer) en reste avec quelqu'un*

    inform: informer v, avertir v

to inform someone of; to put someone in the picture about   *mettre quelqu'un au courant de*

to keep someone informed of   *tenir quelqu'un au courant de*

    information: renseignement m, information f

can you give me some information?   *je peux vous demander un renseignement?*

he has inside information   *il connait tous les dessous*

    infuriate: rendre v furieux

it drives him frantic; it infuriates him   *cela le met hors de lui*

    in hand: en train m, en question f

to have the matter well in hand   *tenir le bon bout*

    inheritance: héritage m

to spend one's inheritance before one gets it   *manger son blé en herbe*

in love: *amoureux,-euse adj*

to fall head over heels in love   *tomber amoureux fou*

innocent: *innocent(e) m,f*

a naïve and innocent person   *un enfant de chœur*

he's no innocent; he wasn't   *il n'est pas tombé de la*
born yesterday   *dernière pluie*

to look so very innocent   *avoir un air de sainte nitouche*

inopportune: *inopportun,-e adj*

to be inopportune; to be out of   *arriver comme un cheveu sur*
place; to happen at the most   *la soupe*
awkward moment

inquiry: *demande f de renseignements*

to make inquiries   *aller aux renseignements*

inside: *dedans adv*

inside and outside; at home   *au dedans et au dehors*
and abroad

inside out: *envers m*

to put on inside out; to turn   *mettre à l'envers*
inside out

interest: *intéresser v*

what are your interests?   *à quoi vous intéressez-vous?*

I am not interested in football   *le football ne m'intéresse pas*

interest: *intérêt m*

it is of interest to (+vb); it is   *il y a intérêt à (+inf)*
desirable to (+vb)

introduce: *présenter v*

have you met my wife?; may I   *je vous présent ma femme*
introduce my wife

invest: *placer v, investir v*

to invest money; to deposit   *placer de l'argent*
money

involve: *entrainer v*

he does not want to get   *il ne veut pas se mouiller*
involved

iron: *repasser v*

to iron under a damp cloth   *repasser à la pattemouille*

J

jam (= *difficulty*): *pétrin m*
to be in the soup; to be in a jam   *être dans le pétrin*
   jest: *plaisanterie f*
he said it in jest   *il l'a dit par plaisanterie*
   jilt: *rompre v avec, laisser tomber v, plaquer v*
she jilted me; she walked out   *elle m'a planté là*
on me
   jitters: *frousse f*
it gives me the jitters   *ça me fiche la trouille*
   joke: *plaisanterie f, blague f*
he's always joking; he's a   *il a toujours le mot pour rire*
born joker
he took our joke in good part   *il a pris notre plaisanterie du*
    bon côté
to tell (or crack) a joke   *faire une plaisanterie*
   joy: *joie f*
to be beside oneself with joy   *ne pas (ou ne plus) se sentir*
    de joie
to be full of the joys of living   *être plein de joie de vivre*
   judge: *juger v*
as far as I can judge; as far as I   *autant que je puisse en juger*
can make out
judging from appearances   *à en juger d'après les*
    apparences

   jump: *sauter v*
to jump about   *sauter de-ci de-là*
to jump at the chance; to seize   *sauter sur l'occase*
the opportunity
to jump on the bandwagon   *monter dans le train en*
    marche; prendre le train en
    marche; suivre le mouvement

   juncture: *jointure f*
at this juncture; at that moment   *sur ces entrefaites; à ce*
    moment-là
   just: *juste adv, de justesse adv*
just the same   *ce n'est pas pour dire, mais*

to be busy doing something;   *être en train de faire quelque*
to be just in the middle of doing   *chose*
something

K

keen: *enthousiaste* adj
I'm not keen on the idea; it   *ça ne me dit rien*
doesn't appeal to me at all
I'm not keen on the idea   *ça ne me chante pas*
to be very keen   *être tout feu tout flamme*
keep: *garder* v
to keep a straight face   *garder son sérieux*
to keep something for a rainy   *garder une poire pour la soif*
day
to keep up appearances   *pour sauver les apparences*
keep: *tenir* v
to keep at a distance (or at   *tenir à distance*
arm's length)
to keep a dog on a lead   *tenir un chien en laisse*
key: *clef, clé* f
to put under lock and key   *mettre sous clef*
kill: *tuer* v
killed on the spot; killed outright   *tué sur le coup*
to kill the goose that lays the   *tuer la poule aux œufs d'or*
golden eggs
to kill two birds with one stone   *faire coup double*
kind: *aimable* adj, *gentil,-ille* adj
he was kind enough to say   *il a eu l'amabilité de dire*
that is very kind of you   *c'est très aimable (ou gentil)*
    à vous
kind: *genre* m, *espèce* f, *sorte* f, *type* m
of all kinds; of every shape and   *de tout poil*
size
what kind of man is he?   *quel genre (ou type)*
    d'homme est-ce?
kindness: *bonté* f
have the kindness to   *ayez la bonté de*

knack: *tour m de main, truc m*

he has found the knack of doing
something
*il a acquis le tour de main
pour faire*

to get the hang (or knack) of
something
*attraper le coup; attraper le
tour de main*

to have the knack
avoir le truc

knickers: *culotte f*

to get one's knickers in a twist
*s'embrouiller (ou s'empétrer)
de belle façon*

knock down: *abattre v*

you could have knocked me
down with a feather
j'en suis resté baba

know: *connaître v, savoir v*

does he know?; is he informed?
est-il au fait?

had I known; if I had known
si j'avais su

I didn't know how right I was
je ne croyais pas si bien dire

I don't know how to set about
it
*je ne sais comment m'y
prendre*

I know him by name
je le connais de nom

I know him by sight
je le connais de vue

not as far as I know; not to my
knowledge
pas que je sache

to be in the know; to know
the ropes
être dans le bain

to be in the know
*être au courant; être au
parfum*

to be known by the name of
être connu sous le nom de

to have information of; to know
about; to be well-informed on
être au courant de

to know a thing or two
en connaître un bout

to know for certain that
savoir à n'en pas douter que

to know how to behave; to
know how to live
savoir vivre

to know it inside out; to be
really clued up about it
en connaître un rayon

to know it to one's cost; to
learn the hard way
être payé pour le savoir

to know the score
connaître la musique

know-how: *savoir-faire m*

know-how; ability; tact
savoir-faire

knowledge: *connaissance f*

he knows what he is talking about; he has full knowledge of the facts	*il parle en connaissance de cause*
that's common knowledge	*c'est de notoriété publique*
to become acquainted with; to obtain knowledge of	*faire connaissance avec*
without my knowledge; without my knowing	*à mon insu*

knuckle under: *céder v*

to knuckle under; to give in; to give up	*mettre les pouces*

L

lack: *manquer v de*

he lacks courage	*le courage lui manque; il manque de courage*

lap up: *laper v*

to lap it up (praise); to feel pleased with oneself	*boire du petit lait*

last resort: *pis-aller m, inv*

that would be a last resort (or stopgap)	*ce serait un pis-aller*

late: *tard adv*

at the latest	*au plus tard*
better late than never	*mieux vaut tard que jamais*
it's getting late	*il commence à se faire tard; il se fait tard*

later: *plus tard adv*

a few moments later	*quelques instants plus tard*

laugh: *rire v*

he was bubbling over with laughter	*il se pouffait de rire*
it's no laughing matter	*il n'y a pas de quoi rire*
to be the laughing stock of	*être la risée de*
to laugh on the other side of one's face	*rire jaune*

to laugh up one's sleeve; to have a quiet laugh	*rire en cachette; rire dans sa barbe; rire sous cape*
to roar with laughter; to laugh outright	*rire à gorge déployée*
to roar with laughter	*rire aux éclats*

launch: *lancer v*

to launch a boat	*lancer un bateau*
to put to sea; to launch a boat	*mettre à la mer; prendre la mer*

lay (table): *mettre v le couvert*

to lay the cloth; to set the table	*mettre le couvert*

lay down: *coucher v*

lying flat on the ground	*couché à plat sur le sol*
lying full in the sun	*couché en plein soleil*

lazy: *paresseux,-euse adj*

to have a lazy streak; to be work-shy	*avoir un poil dans la main*

leaf: *feuille f*

he has turned over a new leaf	*il a fait peau neuve*
you must turn over a new leaf; you must mend your ways	*il faut changer de conduite*

lean over: *se pencher v*

to lean over backwards to help someone	*se mettre (ou se plier) en quatre pour aider quelqu'un*

leapfrog: *dépasser v*

to leapfrog over (a person)	*sauter à saute-mouton par-dessus*

least/most: *le moins (de) adj/le plus (de) adj*

at the very least/at the very most	*tout au moins/tout au plus*

least: *au moins prep*

at the very least; at the lowest estimate	*au bas mot*

leave: *congé m*

to take a week off; to take a week's leave	*prendre un congé d'une semaine*
to take leave of someone	*prendre congé de quelqu'un*

leave: *laisser v, ficher v*

leave it to me	*laissez moi faire*
leave me alone	*fiche-moi le paix*

leave me alone; leave me in peace; don't worry me	*laissez moi tranquil*
to be nonplussed; to be left in the lurch	*rester le bec dans l'eau*
leg: *jambe f*	
to get a rise out of someone; to pull someone's leg	*faire marcher quelqu'un*
leisure: *loisir m*	
at one's leisure	*à tête reposée*
lend: *prêter v*	
could you lend me your umbrella?	*pourriez-vous me prêter votre parapluie?*
length: *long m, longueur f*	
in great detail; at great length	*en long et en large*
to fall at full length; to measure one's length	*tomber tout au long*
less: *moins adv*	
all the less; even less	*d'autant moins*
let: *laisser v*	
to let nature take its course	*laisser agir la nature*
let me do as I like	*laissez-moi faire à ma guise*
let go: *lâcher v*	
to let go; to loosen one's grip	*lâcher prise*
to let the cat out of the bag; to come clean	*lâcher le morceau*
lie: *mensonge m*	
it sounds to me like a lie	*ça m'a l'air d'un mensonge*
lie: *mentir v*	
he is a born liar	*il ment comme il respire*
lie in: *rester v au lit*	
to lie in bed late; to have a long lie in	*dormir (ou faire) la grasse matinée*
life: *vie f*	
at the prime of life; in one's prime	*à la fleur de l'âge*
his life hangs by a thread	*sa vie ne tient qu'à un fil*
in the prime of life	*dans la force de l'âge*
not on your life!; never!	*jamais de la vie!*
lifetime: *vie f, vivant m*	
in his lifetime	*de son vivant*

live

    light: *lumière f*

to go out like a light; to fall asleep instantly	*s'endormir (ou tomber) comme une masse*
to stand in someone's light	*cacher le jour à quelqu'un*

    lightning: *foudre f*

flash of lightning; unexpected event; love at first sight	*coup de foudre*
struck by lightning	*frappé par la foudre*
the church was struck by lightning	*la foudre tombée sur l'eglise*

    like (to be): *on dirait de*

it looks like salmon; it tastes like salmon	*on dirait du saumon*
it's like silk; it feels like silk; it looks like silk	*on dirait de la soie*

    like: *aimer v*

I like that; I fancy that; that suits me down to the ground	*ça me botte*
to like good food; to be fond of good living	*aimer la table*

    likely: *vraisemblablement adv*

most likely; very likely	*vraisemblablement*
probably not	*vraisemblablement pas*

    limp: *boiter v, claudiquer v*

to limp along; to hobble along	*aller (ou marcher) clopin-clopant*

    liquor: *spiritueux m, alcool m*

he can hold his liquor!	*il sait boire!*

    lisp: *zézayer v; zozoter v*

to lisp	*avoir un cheveu sur la langue*

    live: *habiter v*

I live in Yorkshire (in Great Britain)	*j'habite dans le Yorkshire (en Grande Bretagne)*
we live next door to each other	*nous habitons porte à porte*

    live: *vivre v*

to live from hand to mouth	*vivre au jour le jour*
to live in the lap of luxury	*vivre au sein du luxe*
to live it up; to make a scene; to kick up a row	*faire la vie*
to live off; to sponge off	*vivre aux crochets de*

long run: *longue f*
in the long run

à la longue

long time: *longtemps adv*
are you going to be long?

vous en avez pour
longtemps?

he has been living here for a
long time

il habite ici depuis longtemps

j'habite là d ———— long Gang

I shall not be long in getting
dressed

je ne tarderai guère à
m'habiller

that was a long, long while ago;
that was donkey's years ago

il y a belle lurette de cela

look: *coup m d'œil*
he is keeping a sharp look out

il a l'œil au guet

to take a quick look at the
children

jeter un coup d'œil sur les
enfants

vous avez bonne

look: *mine f*
how does she look? she looks
well

quelle mine a-t-elle? elle a
bonne mine

mine

you do not look well

tu n'as pas bonne mine

look: *paraître v, sembler v*
to look surprised; to stare in
amazement

ouvrir de grands yeux

look: *regard m, air m*
to put on a knowing look

prendre un air entendu

look: *regarder v*
I looked him in the face

je le regardais en face

to look askance at; to give a
dirty look

regarder de travers

to look someone up and down

regarder quelqu'un de haut en
bas

look for: *chercher v*
to be on the look out for
something

être à l'affût de quelque
chose

to look for a needle in a
haystack

chercher une aiguille dans
une botte de foin

to look for difficulties; to look
for complications; to complicate
the issue

chercher midi à quatorze
heures

lose: *perdre v*

I'm done for!; it's all up with me! — *je suis perdu!*

to lose ground — *perdre (ou céder) du terrain*

to lose one's balance — *perdre l'équilibre*

loss: *perte f*

to go under; to be ruined; to make a big loss — *boire un bouillon*

to suffer a loss; to get one's fingers burnt — *y laisser des plumes*

lot: *beaucoup adv*

to have a lot to do — *avoir du pain sur la planche*

love: *aimer v, adorer v*

I love cream and custard pastry — *j'adore le millefeuille*

love: *amour m*

I am rather enamoured of her — *je me suis épris d'elle*

it is a love affair — *c'est une affaire du cœur*

to be crazy about; to love to distraction — *aimer à la folie*

to be in love with; to be enamoured with — *être amoureux de*

to fall in love with — *tomber amoureux de*

low: *bas, basse adj*

to be very low; to be at a low ebb — *être au plus bas*

luck: *chance f, hasard m, veine f*

a stroke of luck; a stroke of good fortune — *un hasard heureux*

as luck would have it; by a stroke of luck — *par un coup de chance; par un coup de veine* / fluke

it brings bad luck; it brings misfortune — *cela porte malheur*

it brings good luck; it brings good fortune — *cela porte bonheur; cela porte chance*

you're lucky — *vous avez de la chance; tu a de la chance*

what luck!; how lucky! — *quelle chance!*

lucky: *veinard,-e adj, favorisé par la chance*

I carry my lucky charm everywhere I go — *je porte mon porte-bonheur partout où je vais*

to be born lucky	*être né coiffé*
to be lucky; to have a winning streak	*avoir de la veine*

Quelle veine!

What luck!

M

mad: *fou, fol, folle adj*	
to make someone hopping mad	*faire bondir quelqu'un*
madness: *folie f*	
he is a little mad	*il a un grain de folie*
main thing: *l'essentiel m*	
the main (or chief) thing is to	*l'essentiel, c'est de (+inf)*
make: *faire v*	
it's make or break	*il faut que ça passe ou ça casse*
make do: *s'arranger v*	
to make do with; to put up with	*s'arranger de*
make for: *aller v vers, se diriger v vers*	
to make one's way towards; to make for	*diriger ses pas vers*
make up (one's face): *se maquiller v*	
she made up before the dance	*elle s'est maquillée avant la danse*
make up (one's mind): *prendre v la décision*	
my mind is made up	*c'est tout réfléchi*
man: *homme m*	
a ladies' man	*un homme à bonnes fortunes*
the average man; the man in the street	*l'homme moyen*
manage: *conduire v, mener v, arranger v*	
to manage one's affairs well	*bien conduire (ou mener) sa barque*
to manage to; to get through; to overcome	*venir à bout de*
manner: *manière f, façon f*	
in an unexpected manner	*de façon inopinée*
in such a manner; in that fashion; in that way	*de la sorte*
she has an easy manner	*elle a l'air aisé*

mark: *marque f*

to be up to the mark; to be equal to — *être à la hauteur*

marriage: *mariage m*

he has married into money — *il a fait un riche mariage*

he proposed to her — *il lui a fait une demande en mariage*

marry: *marier v*

to marry for love — *faire un mariage d'inclination (ou d'amour)*

match: *assortir v*

they are an ill-matched couple — *les époux sont mal assorti*

matter: *importer v*

it matters little that; it is not very important that — *il importe peu que*

it matters little whether — *peu importe que*

no matter; never mind; it doesn't matter — *n'importe*

what does it matter? — *qu'importe?*

matter: *matière f*

to get to the heart of the matter — *entrer dans le vif du sujet*

to make matters worse; to crown everything — *pour comble de malheur*

maybe: *peut-être adv*

it may well be; maybe so, maybe not — *peut-être bien*

mean: *vouloir v dire*

do you really mean it? — *c'est pour de vrai?*

what does that mean?; what does that imply? — *qu'est-ce que cela veut dire?*

means: *moyens mpl, revenus mpl*

by fair means or foul; by hook or by crook; by every way possible — *par tous les moyens*

to live within one's means — *mesurer sa dépense à ses revenus; vivre selon ses moyens*

with every means at his disposal — *de tous les moyens dont il dispose*

meanwhile: *en attendant adv*, *pendant ce temps adv*

meanwhile; in the meantime;   *en attendant*
all the same

meet: *rencontrer v*

I'm very pleased to meet you   *enchanté de vous connaître*

there's more to it than meets   *il y a quelque chose*
the eye   *là-dessous*

to meet one's match   *trouver à qui parler*

mention: *mentionner v*

don't mention it; don't speak   *n'en parlez pas*
about it

don't mention it; not at all;   *il n'y a pas de quoi*
you're welcome

not to mention; to say nothing   *sans parler de*
of; let alone

not to mention; not counting   *sans compter*

mere, merely: *rien que adv*

the mere (or very) thought of   *rien que d'y penser (ou*
it makes me shiver   *songer) me fait frissonner*

mess: *gâchis m*, *pétrin m*

a fine mess you are in   *vous voilà dans de beaux*
   draps

they have made a fine mess of   *ils ont fait un beau gâchis de*
this job   *ce travail*

midday: *midi m*

about midday; about lunchtime   *vers midi*

middling: *moyennement adv*

so-so; fair to middling   *comme ci comme ça;*
   couci-couça

midnight: *minuit m*

on the stroke of midnight   *sur le coup de minuit*

mind: *ennuyer v*

make yourself at home!; don't   *ne vous gênez pas!*
mind me

mind: *esprit m*

I gave him a piece of my mind   *je lui ai dit son fait*

never mind that; that's no   *qu'à cela ne tienne*
problem

that puts me in mind of   *cela me rappelle*

to be unable to make up one's mind	*être comme l'âne de Buridan*
minute: minute *f*	
it will only take a minute	*c'est l'affaire d'une minute*
mischief: fredaine *f*, malice *f*, sottises *fpl*	
to be up to mischief; to sow one's wild oats	*faire des fredaines*
to get into mischief; to do stupid things	*faire des bêtises*
misfortune: malheur *m*, malchance *f*	
a stroke of bad luck; a stroke of misfortune	*un hasard malheureux*
he's had a lot of bad luck	*il a eu beaucoup de malchance*
miss: manquer *v*	
I miss him very much	*il me manque beaucoup*
mistake: erreur *f*, faute *f*	
my mistake!	*au temps pour moi!*
mistaken (be): se tromper *v*, se méprendre *v*	
he got it well and truly wrong	*il s'est bel et bien trompé*
I must have made a mistake	*je m'étais sûrement trompé*
there is no mistaking it	*il n'y a pas à s'y méprendre*
to be mistaken; to be on the wrong track; to be kidding oneself	*se mettre le doigt dans l'œil*
unless I am mistaken	*si je ne me trompe*
moment: moment *m*, instant *m*	
at any moment	*à tout moment*
at the moment; at this time; at present	*en ce moment*
for a moment; at the time	*sur le moment*
from that moment	*à partir de cet instant*
from the moment I saw him; as soon as I saw him	*dès l'instant où je l'ai vu*
I don't doubt it for a single moment	*je n'en doute pas un seul instant*
I expect him to arrive any moment now	*j'attends son arrivée d'un moment à l'autre*
money: argent *m*, galette *f* (colloq)	
have you got any money?	*avez-vous de la galette?*

he is rolling in money	il est tout cousu d'or
to get one's money's worth	en avoir pour son argent
to make a pile of money	gagner un argent fou
month: mois m	
a month of Sundays	la semaine de quatre jeudis
mood: humeur f	
to be in a good/bad mood	être bien/mal luné; être de bon/mauvais poil*; être de bonne/mauvaise humeur
moon: lune f	
in the moonlight	au clair de lune
once in a blue moon	tous les trente-six du mois
more: plus adv	
all the more	d'autant plus
all the more so since (or because)	d'autant que; d'autant plus que
furthermore	de plus; en outre
more and more	de plus en plus
moreover: de plus adv	
moreover; what is more	par surcroît; de surcroît
morning: matin m	
very early in the morning	de bon matin; de grand matin
mountain: montagne f	
to make a mountain out of a molehill	se faire une montagne de rien
mouth: bouche f	
to give someone the kiss of life; to give mouth to mouth resuscitation	faire de bouche à bouche à quelqu'un
move: remuer v, déplacer v	
to move heaven and earth to; to leave no stone unturned	remuer ciel et terre pour
much: beacoup adv	
it's a bit much!; that's a bit too much!; that's going a bit too far!	c'est un peu fort!
that's a bit much!	ça alors, c'est quelque chose!
much: grand-chose pron	
there's not much that anyone can do about it	personne n'y peut grand-chose

necessary

we don't know much about it	on ne sait grand-chose à ce sujet

much (as): *autant adv*
as much again
encore autant

much (so): *tellement adv*
he does not work that much
il ne travaille pas tellement

mum (keep): *ne pas piper v mot*
mum's the word!
ni vu ni connu!

mumble: *marmotter v*
stop mumbling
arrête de marmotter; arrête de parler entre tes dents

Si on marmotte
Si on parle entre ses dents
N
je ne tends pa
je ne peux pas entendre

nail: *clou m*
to put one's finger on it; to hit the nail on the head
mettre le doigt dessus

naked: *nu,-e adj*
starkers; in one's birthday suit; naked
à poil

je fais un petit somme
nap: *somme m*
to take a nap; to have forty winks
faire un petit somme
après déjeuner
& après le diner

nasty: *méchant adj*
to turn nasty (or spiteful)
devenir méchant

near: *auprès prep*
he stayed near (or close to) his wife
il restait auprès de sa femme

near: *près adv*
near to; closely
de près

necessary (be): *falloir v*
it is necessary to (+vb); we must (+vb) (e.g. leave)
il faut (+inf) (ex. partir)
one needs courage to do that
il faut du courage pour faire ça
what did you have to do ?
que vous fallait-il faire?

necessary: *nécessaire adj*
it needs to be done; it's necessary to do it
il est nécessaire de le faire

neck: *cou m*

even; game all; neck and neck — *à égalité; manche à manche*

need: *besoin m*

if need be; if necessary — *au besoin*

if the need arises; in case of necessity — *en cas de besoin*

need I tell you? — *est-il besoin de vous dire?*

to need something; to be in need of something — *avoir besoin de quelque chose*

neighbourhood: *voisinage m, quartier m*

about; in the neighbourhood of; in the vicinity of — *aux environs de*

never: *ne jamais adv*

I have never in my life (found, seen, etc) — *je n'ai jamais de ma vie (trouvé, vu etc)*

news: *l'actualité f, les actualités fpl, nouvelle(s) f, fpl*

have you heard the news? — *vous connaissez la nouvelle?*

I should like to have news of him — *je voudrais bien avoir de ses nouvelles*

sports news — *l'actualité sportive*

stop-press news — *nouvelles de dernière heure*

to discuss the latest news — *discuter de l'actualité*

what's your news? — *quoi de neuf chez vous?*

when is the television news? — *les actualités télévisées sont à quelle heure?*

when is the television (radio) news? — *à quelle heure est le journal télévisé (parlé)?*

neck and neck

nothing

New Year: nouvel an m, nouvelle année f

Happy New Year!   bonne année!

next: prochain,-e adj

the next moment he was gone   l'instant d'après il était parti

next to last: avant-dernier m, avant-dernière f

he was the last but one   il était l'avant-dernier

night: nuit f

far into the night; in the small   fort avant dans la nuit
hours of the morning

I had a sleepless night   j'ai passé une nuit blanche
                                (ou nuit sans sommeil)

no: nul, nulle adj

no one else except me knows   nul autre que moi ne le sait
of it

noise: bruit m

an excruciating noise; an ear-   un bruit à vous fendre la tête
splitting noise   (ou les oreilles)

nonsense: absurdités fpl, sottises fpl

nonsense!; you're joking!   et avec ça!

what nonsense!   quelle bêtise!

no one: personne pron

no one else   aucun autre

nose: nez m

he talks through his nose   il parle du nez

to do something under   faire quelque chose à la barbe
someone's nose   de quelqu'un

to thumb one's nose; to cock   faire un pied de nez
a snook

to turn up one's nose at; to   faire fi de
snap one's fingers at

note: noter v, prendre v acte de

duly noted   dont acte

nothing: rien pron

as if nothing had happened   comme si de rien n'était

for next to nothing; very cheaply   pour trois fois rien

he has had no hand in the affair;   il n'a été pour rien dans
he had nothing to do with the   l'affaire
affair

nothing: *rien m*

to have lost everything; to be
left with nothing
*n'avoir plus que ses yeux
pour pleurer*

now: *maintenant adv*

it's now or never
c'est le cas ou jamais

nuisance: *ennui m*

what a nuisance!; what a drag!
quelle barbe!

number: *numéro m*

his number is up!
son affaire est faite

O

26/1

oar: *aviron m, rame f*

to put one's oar in
mettre son grain de sel

oat(s): *avoine f*

to sow one's wild oats
semer sa folle avoine

obsession: *obsession f*

to have an obsession
avoir l'idée fixe

obvious: *évident adj, manifeste adj*

it's obvious; it's self-evident;
it stands to reason
cela tombe sous le sens

that is quite obvious; that sticks
out a mile
cela saute aux yeux

occur: *arriver v*

it occurred to me that
il m'est venu à l'idée que

off-colour: *mal fichu adj*

he is out of sorts; he's a bit
off-colour
il n'est pas dans son assiette

he's off-colour today
il est mal fichu aujourd'hui

oldish: *assez vieux adj*

oldish; getting on; middle-aged
d'un certain âge

one: *un, une adj*

it amounts to one and the same
thing; it's all the same
c'est tout un

on that: *là-dessus adv*

you can count on that
tu peux compter là-dessus

open (candid): *franc, franche adj*

be frank, don't lie!
sois franc, ne mens pas!

to be open-hearted
avoir le cœur sur les lèvres

Note opportunité { opportuneness
expediency
as well as
favourables
= opportunity

overcome

to go about it openly; to be straightforward about it	*y aller de franc jeu*
open: *ouvrir* v	
to keep one's ears open	*avoir l'oreille aux aguets*
open air (in the): *au grand air* m, *en plein air* m	
to sleep out in the open air	*coucher (ou dormir) à la belle étoile*
opinion: *avis* m	
in my opinion	*à mon avis*
opportunity: *occasion* f	
at every opportunity	*à tout propos*
at the first opportunity; at your earliest convenience	*à la première occasion*
to have every opportunity to	*avoir beau jeu de*
opposite: *en face* f	
our neighbours opposite	*nos voisins d'en face*
ordained (be): *être* v *ordonné*	
to be ordained; to enter the Church	*entrer dans les ordres*
to be ordained; to take Holy Orders	*recevoir les ordres*
others: *autres* pron	
the like of us; we (emph)	*nous autres*
outdated: *démodé,-e* adj *suranné,-e* adj, *désuet,-ète* adj	
that's all out-of-date!	*c'est dépassé tout ça!*
this model is out-of-date (or old-fashioned)	*ce modèle est démodé*
to be out-of-date; to be out of fashion	*être suranné*
outlive: *survivre à* v	
she outlived her husband	*elle a survécu à son mari*
outside: *dehors* adv	
outside; irrelevant to; apart from	*en dehors*
that cannot be seen from outside	*cela ne se voit pas de dehors*
overcome: *obvier* v, *parer* v	
to overcome a difficulty (or snag)	*obvier (ou parer) à un inconvénient*
overcome: *succomber* v	
she is overcome by the heat	*elle est abattue par la chaleur*

overdo: *exagérer* v
to go too far; to overdo it — *forcer la dose*

overhear: *surprendre* v
I've overheard a very strange conversation — *j'ai surpris une conversation très curieuse*

over there: *là-bas* adv
look over there — *regardez là-bas*

own: *posséder* v
to own land — *avoir du bien au soleil*

own: *propre* adj
to succeed by one's own efforts — *réussir par ses propres moyens*

P

pace: *marcher* v *à pas mesurés*
to keep pace with — *avancer au même rythme que*

pack: *empaqueter* v, *faire* v *sa valise*
to pack up and go; to get out; to clear off — *plier bagage*

to send someone packing — *envoyer quelqu'un sur les roses* *

paper (daily): *quotidien* m
I take a daily paper — *je suis abonné à un quotidien*

part: *partie* f
to be an integral part of; to be part and parcel of — *faire partie intégrant de*

part: *rôle* m
to play a leading part in; to be the main factor in — *jouer un rôle prépondérant dans*

to play a part; to act a role — *jouer un rôle*

what part did he play in this business? — *quel a été son rôle dans cette affaire?*

particularly: *surtout* adv
I particularly like romantic novels — *j'aime surtout les romans d'amour*

parting: *raie* f *(cheveux)*
to part one's hair — *se faire une raie*

pass: *être reçu* v *(examen)*
to pass an examination — *être reçu à un examen*

pass: *passer v*

in passing; by the way   *en passant*

to pass to and fro   *passer et repasser*

    past: *passé m*

in the deep, dark past; in the mists of time   *dans la nuit des temps*

    path: *chemin m*

I took a short cut; I took a path across the fields   *j'ai pris un chemin de traverse*

    patience: *patience f*   *en doit prendre patience*

to have patience; to be patient   *prendre (ou s'armer de) patience*

    pay: *payer v, régler v*

I have paid the bill   *j'ai réglé la note*

I'll make him pay for that!   *il me le paiera cher!*

the question is settled, no more talk!   *la question est réglée, n'en parlons plus!*

to pay the penalty for; to suffer for; to be punished for   *porter la peine de*

to pay through the nose for   *acheter à prix d'or*

    peculiar: *spécifique adj, propre adj*

the customs peculiar to (or characteristic of) certain regions   *les coutumes propre à certaines regions*

    pension: *retraite f, pension f*

to receive a small pension   *toucher (ou percevoir) une petite retraite*

    people: *gens mpl*

people from all walks of life   *des gens de toutes les conditions (ou de tous les milieux)*

    perfect: *parfaire v, achever v*

to perfect; to finalize; to settle   *mettre au point*

    person: *personne f, individu m*

I'm not that sort of person   *je ne suis pas celle que vous croyez*

    perspire: *transpirer v, suer v*

I am perspiring   *je suis en nage (ou en sueur)*

to begin to perspire; to get into a lather   *se mettre en nage*

persuade: *persuader v*
to need a lot of persauding; to drag one's heels — *se faire tirer l'oreille*

pest: *casse-pieds m,f inv*
he is an absolute pest; he's a pain in the neck — *il me casse les pieds*

pick on: *harceler v*
to pick on; to take it out on; to lay blame on — *s'en prendre à*

picture: *tableau m, image f*
to put someone in the picture; to incriminate someone — *mettre quelqu'un dans le bain*

pig: *cochon m*
when pigs can fly — *quand les poules auront des dents*

pile: *fortune f*
to make one's pile; to feather one's nest — *faire son beurre*

pillion: *tansad m*
back seat; pillion seat — *siège arrière*

pinch (shoes): *serrer v*
that's where the shoe pinches — *c'est là où le bât le blesse*

pin: *épingle f*
he has pins and needles in his legs — *il a des fourmis dans les jambes*

pitch (a story): *débiter v*
to pitch someone a long yarn — *tirer une carotte de longueur à quelqu'un*

pitch: *tomber v sur*
to pitch into someone — *tomber sur quelqu'un à bras raccourcis*

pity: *pitié f*
to take pity on someone — *prendre quelqu'un en pitié*
what a pity!; how unfortunate!; what a tragedy! — *quel malheur!*
what a pity!; what a shame! — *quel dommage!; c'est dommage!*

place: *lieu m, place f*
to take place — *avoir lieu*

plunge

if I were you; if I were in
your place

si j'étais à votre place

plainly: clairement *adv*

to speak plainly

parler sans ambiguïté; parler
sans détours

play: jouer *v*

to play second fiddle to
someone

être le sous-fifre de
quelqu'un

while waiting for him to come
we played cards

en attendant qu'il vienne,
nous jouions aux cartes

please: plaire *v*, faire *v* plaisir

he has it all his own way; he
does as he pleases

il n'en fait qu'à sa tête

to please someone

faire plaisir à quelqu'un

to please someone; to be
agreeable to someone

plaire à quelqu'un

pleasing: avenant,-e *adj*

he has pleasing manners; he
has engaging manners

il a de manières avenantes

pluck: courage *m*

to have pluck

n'avoir pas froid aux yeux

plump: grasouillet,-ette *adj*

he is getting plump

il prend de l'embonpoint

plump; well-padded (person)

bien en chair

plunge: plongeon *m*

to take the plunge

faire le saut; sauter le pas;
sauter le fossé

to take the plunge

point: *point m*

beside the point; off the point	*à côté de la question*
by the way; come to the point!	*au fait!*
it has its good and its bad points; you have to take it with a grain of salt	*il y a à boire et à manger là-dedans*
that's not the point	*la question n'est pas là*
that is not to the point	*cela manque d'à propos*
to go straight to the point	*aller droit au but*
to some degree; up to a point; to a certain extent	*jusqu'à un certain point*

position: *place f, position f, qualité f*

in his capacity (or position) as manager	*en sa qualité de directeur*
put yourself in my position	*mettez-vous à ma place*
to be in a position to (+vb); to be able to (+vb)	*être à même de (+inf)*
you are in a strong position; it's all plain sailing	*vous êtes en bonne passe*

possible: *possible adj*

as far as possible	*dans la mesure du possible*
if possible I should like to visit the opera	*si possible je voudrais aller à l'opéra*
it is possible that	*il se peut que* it may be
you don't say!; well I never!; that's impossible!	*c'est pas possible!*

post: *poste f, courrier m (lettres)*

by return of post	*par retour du courrier*
by the next post	*par le prochain courrier*
sent by post; posted	*envoyé (ou expédié ou mise) à la poste*

postpone: *remettre v, renvoyer v*

to postpone a matter; to let a matter stand over	*remettre une affaire à plus tard*

practice: *habitude f, pratique f*

to become a way of life; to become normal practice	*entrer dans les mœurs*

predicament: *embarras m*

to get into difficulties; to get into a predicament	*se mettre dans l'embarras*

prefer: préférer *v*

I prefer reading a science-fiction novel — *je préfère lire un roman de science-fiction*

do you prefer tea or coffee to drink? — *vous préférez boire du thé ou du café?*

would rather; would sooner; would prefer to — *aimer mieux (+inf)*

preference: préférence *f*

in preference to; rather than — *de préférence à*

present: actuel,-elle *adj*

at the present time — *à l'heure actuelle*

in the world of today one can find — *dans le monde actuel on peut trouver .*

press-up: traction *f*, pompe *f*

to do press-ups (or push-ups) — *faire des pompes; faire des tractions*

pretend: faire *v* semblant

he is pretending to be ill — *il fait le malade*

to pretend to (+vb) — *faire semblant de (+inf)*

prevail: prévaloir *v* sur, l'emporter *v*

to get the better of; to prevail over — *l'emporter sur*

prevaricate: tergiverser *v*

to beat around the bush — *y aller par quatre chemins*

previously: auparavant *adv*

just previously — *quelques instants auparavant*

prey: proie *f*

to fall (or become) prey to — *devenir la proie de*

price: prix *m*

at the lowest price; at rock-bottom price — *au plus juste prix*

price-list — *prix courant; tarif*

prices being what they are — *aux prix où est le beurre*

private: privé,-e *adj*

can I speak to you in private? — *est-ce que je peux vous parler en privé?*

probability: probabilité *f*

in all probability; in all likelihood — *selon toutes probabilités; selon toute vraisemblance*

proceedings (legal): *procès m*
to bring an action against; to   *intenter un procès à*
start proceedings against
progress: *progrès m*
you are improving   *vous êtes en progrès*
you are making progress; you   *vous faites des progrès*
are improving
promise: *promesse f*
to keep one's promise   *tenir sa promesse*
proof: *preuve f*
it's a clear sign; it's clear proof   *c'est un signe qui ne trompe*
   pas

proportion: *proportion f*
as; (proportionally) as; as soon   *à mesure que; au fur et à*
as   *mesure que*
the time will be increased   *le temps sera augmenté*
accordingly (or in the same   *d'autant*
proportion)
protest: *protester v*
I protested for all I was worth   *j'ai protesté comme un beau*
   diable

prove: *prouver v*
to prove fatal to our plans   *porter le dernier coup (ou le*
   coup fatal) à nos projets
to prove to be ambitious; to   *se révéler (comme) ambitieux*
show oneself to be ambitious
provided that: *pourvu que conj*
let's hope he comes; provided   *pourvu qu'il vienne*
that he comes; so long as he
comes
prudence: *prudence f*
to use discretion   *agir avec prudence*
pull strings for: *pistonner v*
to get someone to pull strings;   *se faire pistonner*
to get strings pulled
punch: *coup m de poing*
not to pull any punches; to go   *ne pas faire dans la dentelle*
straight in
purpose: *exprès adv, but m, objet m*
for the purpose in hand   *pour les besoins de la cause*

I did it on purpose	*je l'ai fait exprès*
what is the purpose of his (or her) visit	*quel est le but de sa visite?*
with this intention; for that (or this) purpose	*avec (ou dans) cette intention*
to no purpose; fruitlessly; for absolutely nothing	*en pure perte*
push: *pousser v*	
push in the right direction; finishing touches; final touch	*coup de pouce*
to push one's way through the crowd	*se frayer un chemin à travers la foule*
pushover: *un jeu m d'enfant*	
it's a pushover; it's as easy as wink	*c'est du beurre; c'est un vrai beurre*
put: *mettre v*	
to put (or set) a little money aside	*mettre un peu d'argent de côté*
put off: *renvoyer v*	
to put something off indefinitely	*renvoyer (ou remettre) quelque chose aux calendes grecques*
put out: *gêner v, ennuyer v, déranger v*	
if you don't mind; if it won't put you out	*si cela ne vous gêne pas*

Q

The Hill

quality: *qualité f*	
the food is first-rate here; the food is top quality here	*la cuisine est de première qualité ici*
quarrel: *querelle f*	
to pick a quarrel with someone	*chercher querelle à quelqu'un*
quench: *étancher v*	
to quench one's thirst	*étancher sa soif*
question: *question f*	
I would like to ask a question	*je voudrais poser une question*
it's a matter of; it's a question of	*il s'agit de*

it's a matter of thirty francs; it's a question of thirty francs — *il y va de trente francs*

it is a question whether — *c'est à savoir si*

it's out of the question — *il ne faut pas y songer*

out of the question!; not on your life! — *pas question!*

queue: *queue f*

to line up in a queue — *faire la queue*

quicken: *presser v, accélérer v*

to hurry on; to quicken one's pace — *presser le pas (ou l'allure)*

quickly: *vite adv*

as quickly as possible — *au plus vite; le plus vite possible*

R

rack: *se creuser v, se triturer v*

to rack one's brains — *se casser la tête; se triturer les méninges*

radio: *radio f*

it's the time signal on the radio — *c'est le signal horaire à la radio*

on the radio — *à la radio*

turn (or put) on the radio — *mets la radio* *je mets la radio pour écouter Filtes*

rage: *attraction f, fureur f, rage f*

he (or she, or it) is all the rage — *on se l'arrache*

that is all the rage — *cela fait fureur*

rain: *pleuvoir v*

it's raining, just our luck! — *il pleut, on est gâté!*

on rainy days; on days when it rains — *les jours où il pleut*

rate: *taux m*

at the rate of (quantity) — *au taux de* *examples of je subjunctive*

rather: *plutôt adv*

he would rather you did it — *il préfère que ce soit vous qui le fassiez*

I would rather you came yourself — *je préférerais que vous veniez vous-même*

195

she's rather a clever person	*elle est plutôt intelligente*
reach: *arriver v*	
to reach one's journey's end	*arriver à destination*
read: *lire v*	
I read about it in the newspaper	*je l'ai lu dans le journal*
this novel is worth reading	*ce roman mérite d'être lu*
readily: *volontiers adv*	
readily enough	*assez volontiers*
ready: *prêt adj*	
are you ready?; do you follow me?	*tu y es?*
everything is ready	*tout est prêt*
real: *vrai adj*	
for real; really; seriously	*pour de vrai*
realize: *se rendre v compte de*	*je me rends*
without realizing it	*sans s'en rendre compte*
really: *ne guère adv, vraiment adv*	
I really do not know what to do	*je ne sais vraiment pas quoi faire*
it won't really last	*ça ne durera guère*
oh, really?	*oh, quand même?*
really; actually	*en vérité*
that doesn't really suit you	*cela ne te va guère*
rear: *arrière m*	
to bring up the rear	*fermer la marche*
reason: *raison f*	
for my own reasons	*pour des raisons qui m'appartiennent*
for some reason or other	*pour une raison quelconque*
how comes that?; what is the reason that	*d'où vient que*
the reason why	*la raison pour laquelle*
there is no reason to	*il n'y a pas lieu de (+inf)*
to bring someone to his senses; to talk some sense into someone	*mettre quelqu'un à la raison*
receipt: *reçu m*	
on receipt of	*au reçu de*
recharge: *recharger v*	
to recharge one's batteries; to take a well earned rest	*recharger ses accus*

recklessly: *imprudemment* adv

recklessly; without restraint — *à corps perdu*

    reckless person: *casse-cou* m,f.inv

my brother is a reckless fellow — *mon frère est un casse-cou*

    recollect: *souvenir* v

to the best of my recollection — *autant que je m'en souvienne*

    recourse: *recours* m

to have recourse to; to resort to — *avoir recours à*

    reference (to): *quant à* adv

with reference to this; in this connection — *à ce propos*

    refuse: *refuser* v

it would be better to refuse — *il vaudrait mieux refuser*

    regard: *respect* m, *bon souvenir* m

give him my kind regards — *rappelez-moi à son bon souvenir*

give my best regards to — *présentez mes respects à*

    region: *parages* mpl, *région* f

in this region; in these parts — *dans ces parages*

    rein: *bride* f, *rêne* f

to give full play to; to give free rein to — *donner libre carrière (ou cours) à*

    relative: *un(e) parent(e)* m,f *à moi, membre* m *de ma famille*

they are closely related; they are close relatives — *ils sont proches parents*

    relieve (spend a penny): *se soulager* v

to relieve oneself; to spend a penny — *faire ses besoins*

    reluctantly: *à contrecœur* adv

he did it, but reluctantly — *il l'a fait, mais à contrecœur*

    rely: *compter* v *sur, avoir* v *confiance en*

you can rely on me for that — *ça, vous pouvez me faire confiance*

    remain: *rester* v

I have fifty francs left — *il me reste cinquant francs*

it remains to be seen whether — *il reste à savoir si*

    remember: *rappeler* v, *se souvenir* v

as far back as I can remember — *du plus loin qu'il me souvienne*

I do not remember the address	*je ne me rappelle pas l'adresse*
if I remember rightly	*s'il m'en souvient bien; si j'ai bonne mémoire*
remember your promise!	*souviens-toi de ta promesse!*

repair: *réparation f*

the house is under repair	*la maison est en réparation*

reply: *réponse f*

it's tit for tat	*c'est la réponse du berger à la bergère*

report: *procès-verbal m, rapport m*

official report; statement; minutes	*procès-verbal*

report: *rapporter v*

it is reported that; rumour has it that	*le bruit court que*

reprisals: *représailles fpl*

by way of reprisal (for)	*par voie de représailles; en représailles de*

request: *instance f, demande f*

at the earnest request of	*sur les instances pressantes de*

reserve: *arrière-pensée f*

without reserve	*sans arrière-pensée*

resignation: *démission f*

to hand in one's resignation; to resign one's post	*donner sa démission*

respect: *égard m*

in every respect; in all respects	*à tous égards*

respite: *relâche m,f*

without respite; without ceasing	*sans relâche*

responsibility: *responsabilité f*

he assumes (or shoulders) responsibility	*il endosse une responsabilité*

responsible: *responsable adj*

to a large extent he's responsible for it	*il y est pour beaucoup*

retirement: *retraite f*

to retire; to go into retirement	*prendre sa retraite*

to retire early; to take early retirement — *prendre une retraite anticipée*

retirement years: *troisième âge m*   ~~je suis a mon~~

he is in retirement; he has become a senior citizen — *il est arrivé à son troisième âge*

retrace: *rebrousser v chemin*

to retrace one's steps — *revenir sur ses pas*

retrieve: *rétablir v*

to retrieve the situation — *sauver la situation*

return (home): *rentrer v*

he's going back home — *il rentre; il revient chez soi*

he's returned empty-handed — *il est rentré (ou revenu) bredouille; il est rentré les mains vides.*

return: *revenir v, rendre v, retour m*

he has returned; he is back again — *il est de retour*   ~~nous sommes et still je sais~~

in return for; in exchange for — *en retour de*

let us return to the subject — *mais revenons à nos moutons*

on approval; on sale or return — *avec faculté de retour*

to return good for evil — *rendre le bien pour le mal*

to return someone's affection — *payer de retour l'affection de quelqu'un*

returnable: *consigné,-e adj*

non-returnable — *non consigné*

reveal: *révéler v*

to bring to light; to reveal — *mettre au jour*

review: *revue f*

to review; to review in one's mind; to inspect — *passer en revue*

ride: *monter v*

can you ride (a horse)? — *savez-vous monter à cheval?*

to ride a horse — *monter à cheval; faire du cheval*

ridicule: *ridicule adj & m*

to make oneself ridiculous; to become ridiculous — *tomber dans le ridicule*

to ridicule someone — *tourner quelqu'un en ridicule*

right: *bien adj*

he goes the right way about it — *il s'y prend bien*

right: droit m

what right have you to say that?   *de quel droit dites-vous cela?*

right: juste adj & adv

to say just the right thing; to hit the nail on the head   *tomber juste*

you are perfectly right; nothing could be fairer   *rien de plus juste*

right: raison f

that's right; that's it   *c'est ça*

rightly or wrongly   *à tort ou à raison*

to admit someone is right   *donner raison à quelqu'un*

you are right   *tu as raison*

tort

rip-off: arnaque m

it's a rip-off; you pay through the nose   *c'est le coup de fusil; c'est de l'arnaque**

rise: élever v

he has risen as far as he can   *il a son bâton de maréchal*

road: route f

one for the road   *le coup de l'étrier*

roll: liste f

to call the roll; to call out the names   *faire l'appel*

roll: rouler v

to roll on the ground   *rouler par terre*

roof: toit m

to hit the roof; to have a fit   *piquer une crise*

one for the road

room: *pièce f, salle f*

to give a room a dust; to give the dishes a wipe — *donner up coup de torchon (sur)*

room (space): *place f*

there is no room; there isn't a vacancy — *il n'y a pas de place*

there's no room to move — *on n'a pas de place pour se retourner*

root: *clouer v, enraciner v*

to remain rooted (or frozen) to the spot — *rester figé sur place*

rope: *corde f*

to know the ropes — *connaître les ficelles*

row: *tapage m*

to create a din; to cause a furore — *faire du tapage*

ruin: *ruine f*

to go to rack and ruin; to be on the road to ruin; to be falling apart — *aller à vau-l'eau*

rule: *règle f*

you must make your request according to the rules (or proper procedures) — *il faut faire la demande dans (ou selon) les règles*

rumpus: *chahut m*

to create a devil of a rumpus (or shindy) — *faire le diable à quatre*

run: *courir v*

run for your lives!; each one for him/her self! — *sauve-qui-peut!*

to come running up — *arriver au pas de course*

to run along (a path, road) — *parcourir au pas de course*

to run in all directions — *courir en tous sens*

run: *marcher v, fonctionner v*

things are running smoothly; everything is looking great — *ça baigne dans l'huile*

run into: *tomber v sur*

I ran into my old friend — *je suis tombé sur mon viel ami*

    rush: *bousculade f*
he can't get his words out fast   *ça se bouscule au portillon*
enough
    rush: *se précipiter v*
to rush into the room; to burst   *faire irruption dans la pièce*
into the room

S

    sack (dismiss): *renvoyer v*
to get the sack   *être renvoyé*
to sack someone; to turn   *mettre quelqu'un à la porte*
someone out of the house
    sacrifice: *sacrifice m*
to make great sacrifices   *faire de grands sacrifices; se*
     saigner aux quatre veines

    saddle: *imposer v, coller v*
to be saddled with; to be   *avoir sur le dos*
stuck with
    saddle: *selle f*
to be firmly in the saddle   *être bien en selle*
    safe: *en sécurité f*
as an extra precaution; to be   *pour plus de sûreté*
on the safe side
    sail: *voile f*
to set sail; to get under sail   *mettre à la voile; faire voile*
    same: *même adj & adv*
all the same; nevertheless   *tout de même; quand même*
it amounts to the same thing   *cela revient au même*
it comes to the same thing; it   *c'est du pareil au même*
makes no odds
it comes to the same thing; it's   *c'est bonnet blanc et blanc*
six of one and half a dozen of   *bonnet*
of the other
it's all the same; it makes no   *c'est la même chose*
odds
she'll do the same; she'll do   *elle fera de même*
likewise

save: *sauver* v

to save oneself; to save one's skin	*sauver sa peau*

say: *dire* v

as they say	*comme dit l'autre*
he must have said that tongue in cheek	*il a dû le dire en blaguant*
how shall I put it?; what can I say?	*comment dirais-je?*
I must say that you look very well	*je dois dire que tu as très bonne mine*
it is easier said than done	*c'est plus facile à dire qu'à faire*
one might as well say that	*autant vaudrait dire que*
say what you like; say what you will	*on a beau dire*
sorry!, what did you say	*que dites-vous?; vous dites?; qu'est-ce que tu dis?*
that is (to say)	*c'est-à-dire*
that's an exaggeration; that's saying a lot	*c'est beaucoup dire*
that goes without saying	*cela va sans dire*
without saying a word	*sans mot dire*

scent (hunting): *piste* f, *voie* f

to put someone off the scent (or track)	*donner le change à quelqu'un*

scent (perfume): *parfum* m

what a delicate scent (or fragrance)!	*quel parfum délicat!*

scrap: *bagarre* f

clean sweep; clear out; dust-up; scrap	*coup de torchon*

scruple: *scrupule* m

he does not scruple to	*il ne se fait aucun scrupule*

sea-dog: *loup* m *de mer*

he is an old sea-dog (or salt)	*il est un vieux loup de mer*

seal: *sceller* v

my lips are sealed	*je serai un vrai tombeau*

seat (take a): *s'asseoir* v

to take one's seat	*prendre place*

seat: *siège* m

to be in the hot seat; to be on the spot — *être sur la sellette*

second-hand: *occasion* f

I bought it second-hand — *je l'ai acheté d'occasion*

secrecy: *secret* m

with the utmost secrecy — *dans le plus grand secret*

secretly: *secrètement* adv, *en secret* adv

to do something secretly (or on the sly) — *faire quelque chose en sourdine*

see: *voir* v

as far as the eye can see; interminably — *à perte de vue*

he sees the bright side of everything — *il voit tout en rose; il voit tout en beau*

he sees the dark side of everything — *il voit tout en noir*

I can see what you are getting at — *je te vois venir*

I haven't seen you for ages — *il y a un siècle qu'on ne vous a vu*

let's see; let's think; wait and see — *attendez voir*

they'll see what I'm made of! — *on verra de quel bois je me chauffe!*

to see fit to — *trouver bon de*

to see life through rose-coloured spectacles — *voir la vie en rose*

you've never seen the like! — *c'est du jamais vu!*

see again (to): *revoir* v

it's lovely to see you again — *ça fait bien plaisir de vous revoir*

see to: *se charger* v

I will see to it — *je m'en chargerai*

seize: *saisir* v

to seize (or jump at) the opportunity — *saisir (ou prendre) la balle au bond*

seldom: *rarement* adv

seldom; infrequently — *peu souvent*

sell: *vendre* v

anybody interested? I'm selling my bicycle! — *avis aux amateurs, je vend mon vélo!*

to sell/buy for cash — *vendre/acheter au comptant*

send for: *faire* v *venir*

I've sent for the doctor — *j'ai fait venir le médecin*

sense: *sens* m

against all common sense; any old how — *en dépit du sens commun*

separately: *à part* adv, *séparément* adv

to go it alone; to keep to oneself; to form a separate group — *faire bande à part*

seriously: *sérieusement* adv

to take seriously — *prendre au sérieux*

serve: *servir* v

it serves him right — *c'est bien fait pour lui*

setback: *revers* m, *échec* m

to suffer a setback — *remporter une veste*

set on edge: *agacer* v

that sets my teeth on edge — *cela m'agace les dents*

set out: *partir* v

to set out on a journey — *partir en voyage*

settle: *régler* v; *liquider* v

to settle a difference out of court — *régler une affaire à l'amiable*

sex: *sexe* m

a sex scandal; a sex case — *une affaire (ou histoire) de mœurs*

to have a one-track mind; to have sex on the mind — *ne penser qu'à ça*

to have sex on the mind; to be a randy so-and-so — *être porté sur la bagatelle*

shadow: *ombre* f

to be only a shadow of one's former self — *n'être plus que l'ombre de soi-même*

shame: *honte* f

now isn't that a shame! — *le beau malheur!*

to put someone to shame — *faire honte à quelqu'un*

share: *partager v*
I do not share that view — je ne partage pas cette opinion

share: *portion f*
to be down to the bare essentials; to get the smallest share — être réduit à la portion congrue

sharp (time): *précise adj, pile adv*
it's ten (etc) o'clock sharp (or on the dot — il est dix (etc) heures pile

shirk: *esquiver v*
to shirk duty; to malinger — carotter le service

shirt: *chemise f*
in one's shirt-sleeves — en manches (ou bras) de chemise

shoe: *chaussure f*
my shoes let in water — mes chaussures prennent l'eau

shopping: *course(s) f, fpl*
to do some some shopping; to run errands — faire des courses
to go window shopping — lécher les vitrines; faire du lèche-vitrines

short cut: *raccourci m*
to take a short cut — prendre un raccourci

shortly: *peu adv*
shortly after/before — peu après/avant

shot: *coup m*
a wasted effort — un coup d'épée dans l'eau
to go off like a shot — partir comme un trait

shoulder: *épaule f*
to shrug one's shoulders — hausser les épaules

shout: *crier v*
he shouts at the top of his voice; he shouts his head off — il crie à tue-tête

show in: *faire entrer v*
to show someone in — faire entrer quelqu'un

shut up: *fermer v*
to shut up shop; to do a bunk; to clear out — mettre la clef sous la porte

shy: *timide adj*, *réservé adj*
he's ever so slightly reserved;   *il est un tant soit peu*
he's a little bit shy   *réservé*
sick: *malade adj*
he feels sick; he has nausea   *il a mal au cœur* → = not heart
to look really sick; to look down   *avoir (ou faire) une gueule*   attack!
in the mouth   *d'enterrement*
side: *côté m*
side by side; cheek by jowl   *côté à côté*
the other side of the coin; the   *le revers de la medaille*
dark side of the picture
sight (on): *d'emblée adv*
to dislike someone on sight   *détester quelqu'un d'emblée*
sight: *vue f*
at first sight; initially   *au premier abord*
he is short-sighted (or near-   *il a la vue basse (ou courte)*
sighted)
I lost sight of it   *je l'ai perdu de vue*
keeness of sight   *acuité visuelle; acuité de*
    vision

silent: *silencieux,-ieuse adj*
to remain silent; to lie low   *se tenir coi; rester coi;*
    rester silencieux; garder le
    silence

silly: *bête adj & f, idiot,-e adj*
ask a silly question and you'll   *à question idiote, réponse*
get a silly answer   *idiote*
to act silly; to behave foolishly   *faire la bête*
simple: *simple adj*
it's quite simple; it's quite   *c'est tout trouvé*
straightforward
since: *depuis prep, puisque conj*
ever since then; from that   *depuis lors; dès lors*
time on
since   *depuis que; depuis le temps*
    que
seeing that; as long as; since   *du moment que*
sing: *chanter v*
they all sang their best   *ils chantaient à qui mieux*
    mieux

sip: *siroter* v
to sip   *boire à petites gorgées; boire*
                                            à petits coups

sit (exam): *passer* v, *se présenter* v
to sit for an examination   *passer un examen; se*
                                            présenter à un examen

situated: *situer* v
to be situated miles from   *être situé au diable vauvert*
anywhere; to be stuck out in
the countryside

situation; *situation* f
he managed to save the   *il a réussi à sauver la*
situation   *situation*
it's a "daggers drawn" situation   *le torchon brûle*

size: *taille* f
large/small/all sizes   *grandes/petites/toutes tailles*
what size do you take?   *quelle est votre taille?*

skate: *patiner* v
to skate on thin ice; to tread on   *marcher sur des œufs*
delicate ground

skin: *peau* f
to have got someone under   *avoir quelqu'un dans la peau*
one's skin; to be crazy about
someone

slap: *pêche* f
to slap someone across the face   *donner une pêche à*
                                            quelqu'un

slapdash: *sans soin* m
to be slapdash; to be too quick   *aller trop vite en besogne*
off the mark

slate: *ardoise* f
let's let bygones be bygones!;   *passons l'éponge!*
let's forget all about it!; let's
wipe the slate clean!

sleep: *dormir* v
to sleep around   *coucher avec n'importe qui*
to sleep like a log   *dormir comme un loir;*
                                            dormir comme une souche;
                                            dormir à poings fermés;
                                            dormir comme un sabot

to sleep soundly	*dormir sur les deux oreilles*
sleep: *sommeil m*	
to feel sleepy; to be sleepy	*avoir sommeil*
to be a light/heavy sleeper	*avoir le sommeil léger/lourd*
sling: *écharpe f*	
he has his arm in a sling	*il a le bras en écharpe*
slip away: *s'esquiver v, s'éclipser v*	
he gave me the slip; he sneaked away from me	*il m'a faussé compagnie*
to slip away	*partir en tapinois*
slow-witted: *à l'esprit m lent*	
to be very slow on the uptake	*avoir un métro de retard*
slow down: *ralentir v*	
to slacken one's pace; to slow down	*ralentir le pas*
sly: *rusé adj, dissimulé adj, sournois adj*	
a sharp fellow; a sly fellow	*un vert gaillard*
slyly: on the sly; furtively	*en tapinois*
smashing: *formidable adj*	
great; fantastic; smashing; perfection	*au poil; au quart de poil*
smell: *sentir v*	
this tea smells of lemon; this tea tastes of lemon	*ce thé sent le citron*
smile: *sourire m & v*	
she was full of smiles	*elle était toute souriante*
smirk: *petit sourire m satisfait*	
to smirk (in a self-satisfied, or affected way)	*sourire d'un air satisfait (ou affecté)*
smoothly: *facilement adv*	
it is all going smoothly; it is going like clockwork	*ça marche comme sur des roulettes*
smoothly; without conflict	*sans heurts*
snack: *casse-croûte m, inv*	
to have a snack	*manger sur le pouce*
snag: *difficulté f, os m, bec m*	
to find (or hit) a snag	*trouver (ou tomber sur) un os*
there's a snag; there's a hitch	*il y a un os*

sneeze: *éternuer* v

it's not to be sneezed at | ce n'est pas de la petite bière; ce n'est pas à dédaigner; il ne faut pas cracher dessus

so, thus: *ainsi* adv

if that (or such) is the case, I'm leaving | s'il en est ainsi, je m'en vais

so-called: *soi-disant* adj. inv

our so-called (or would-be) poet | notre soi-disant poète

sob: *sanglot* m

to burst into sobs (or tears) | éclater en sanglots

solicit: *racoler* v

to solicit in the streets; to walk the streets | faire le trottoir

solution: *solution* f

there's only one solution | il n'y a pas trente-six solutions

somehow: *d'une façon* f

come what may; after a fashion; somehow | vaille que vaille

sometimes: *parfois* adv

it happens sometimes that | il arrive parfois que

somewhere: *quelque part* adv

put your bag somewhere in the corner | mettez votre valise quelque part dans le coin

soon: *bientôt* adv, *tôt* adv

as soon as; no sooner than | sitôt que; sitôt après

as soon as possible | aussitôt que possible; dans le délai le plus bref

see you soon! | à bientôt!

sooner or later | tôt ou tard

the sooner the better | le plus tôt sera le mieux

sorry (be): *être désolé* v, *regretter* v, *être fâché* v

I am sorry that I cannot help you | je suis fâché de ne pas vous pouvoir aider

I'm sorry, but this table has already been reserved | je regrette, mais cette table a déjà été reservée

I'm sorry to have disturbed you | je suis désolé de vous avoir dérangé

I'm sorry to have kept you waiting	*je regrette de vous avoir fait attendre*
I'm very (or terribly) sorry	*je suis vraiment désolé*
to be in a sorry state; to get into bad ways	*filer un mauvais coton*
sort out: *arranger v, trier v*	
to put things straight; to sort things out	*arranger les choses*
soul: *âme f*	
like a lost soul	*comme une âme en peine*
there wasn't a soul inside	*il n'y avait pas un chat dedans*
sound: *son m*	
I was woken by the sound of bells	*j'étais réveillé par le son des cloches*
sour: *aigre adj*	
to turn sour	*tourner à l'aigre (ou au vinaigre)*
space: *place f*	
to take up a lot of room (or space)	*prendre de la place*
speak: *dire v, parler v*	
he spoke at length about	*il a s'étendu sur*
he spoke his mind	*il a dit son façon de penser*
so to speak; as it were	*pour ainsi dire*
speak at random; to blather	*parler à tort et à travers*
to speak fluently	*parler avec abondance*
to speak frankly	*parler sans ambages*
to speak frankly; to speak plainly	*parler sans détours*
to speak freely; to unbosom oneself	*parler à cœur ouvert*
to speak freely to one another; to have a heart-to-heart talk	*se parler à cœur ouvert*
to speak off the cuff; to extemporize; to speak at length	*parler d'abondance*
to speak up	*parler haut; parler à haute voix*
to take the floor to speak; to commence to speak	*prendre la parole pour dire*

speaker: *interlocuteur m, interlocutrice f, orateur m, oratrice f*

she has a ready tongue; she is   *elle a la parole facile*
a fluent speaker

specially: *spécialement adv*

incomparable; specially made;   *hors série*
custom made

speed: *vitesse f*

at breakneck speed   *à tombeau ouvert*

hell for leather; full tilt; at top   *à fond de train*
speed

to shoot off at high speed; to   *démarrer sur les chapeaux de*
take off like a shot   *roue*

spell: *épeler v, écrire v*

can you spell it for me?   *pouvez-vous me l'épeler?*

how do you spell (or write) it?   *comment est-ce que cela*
    s'écrit?

spicy: *piquant adj, salé adj*

spicy stories   *contes gaillards*

spin: *faire tourner v*

to spin a coin   *faire tourner une pièce de*
    monnaie; jouer à pile ou face

split: *partager v*

to split the difference   *couper la poire en deux*

split hairs: *chinoiser v*

to split hairs; to quibble   *chercher la petite bête;*
    couper les cheveux en quatre

spoilsport: *rabat-joie m,f, inv, gâte-tout m,f, inv*

don't be such a spoilsport   *ne joue pas les rabat-joie (ou*
    les trouble-fête)

he's a spoilsport; he's a muddler   *il est un gâte-tout*

spoke (wheel): *rayon m*

to put a spoke in someone's   *mettre des bâtons dans les*
wheel; to put a spanner in the   *roues à quelqu'un*
works

sponger: *pique-assiette m,f, inv*

he is a sponger (or parasite)   *il est un pique-assiette*

sprain: *entorse f*

to sprain one's ankle   *se donner une entorse; se*
    faire une entorse

spread: *(se) répandre* v

this opinion is gaining ground;
this opinion is spreading
    cette opinion se répand

spree: *fête* f

to have a night out; to go out
on a spree
    *faire la tournée des grands
ducs*

squarely, bluntly: *carrément* adv

he made no bones about it; he
went bluntly to the point
    il y est allé carrément

stamp: *marquer* v

he is a man of the right stamp;
he is a man of commonsense
    il est marqué au bon coin

stand: *se tenir* v

to stand on tiptoe
    *se tenir (ou se dresser) sur la
pointe des pieds*

stand and gape: *bayer* v

to stand gaping; to star gaze
    bayer aux corneilles

stand up: *poser* v

to stand someone up
    poser un lapin à quelqu'un *

stare at: *dévisager* v

I stared him out of countenance
    *je lui ai fait perdre
contenance*

start: *soubresaut* m

the news gave me a start
    *la nouvelle m'a donné un
soubresaut*

starve: *faire* v *souffrir de la faim*

I'm starving*; I'm famished*
    je crève de faim *

state: *affirmer* v

to insist; to state firmly
    affirmer avec force

statement: *exposition* f, *déclaration* f

that's an understatement
    c'est peu dire

stature: *stature* f, *taille* f

he was a man short in stature
    *il était un homme de petite
taille*

stay: *rester* v, *séjourner* v

I stayed at his house
    j'ai séjourné chez lui
to stay in bed
    garder le lit
we can only stay for a few
moments
    *nous ne pouvons rester que
quelques instants*

steal: *dérober v, voler v*

to steal a kiss from someone — *dérober un baiser à quelqu'un*

sting: *piquer v*

to sting someone to the quick — *piquer quelqu'un au vif*

stop: *rester v, arrêter v*

I'm only stopping for a moment — *je ne fais qu'entrer et sortir*

stopping: *arrêt m, cessation f*

they work without stopping — *ils travaillent sans désemparer*

story: *histoire f, récit m*

a cock-and-bull story — *une histoire à dormir debout*

that's another story; that's another way of looking at it — *c'est un autre son de cloche*

that's quite a different matter; that's quite a different story — *ça, c'est une autre chanson*

to give an account of; to tell the story of — *faire le récit de*

straight: *droit,-e adj*

give it to me straight!; don't beat about the bush! — *n'y va pas quatre chemins!*

I got it straight from the horse's mouth — *je le tiens de bonne source*

straight off: *sans hésiter v*

to do something straight off; to do something at a moment's notice — *faire quelque chose au pied levé*

strain (to do): *peiner v pour faire*

to strain every nerve to; to do anything for — *se mettre en quatre pour (+inf)*

strange thing: *curieux m*

the strange thing is that — *le plus curieux, c'est que*

straw: *paille f*

that's the last straw!; that's going too far! — *c'en est trop!*

strength: *force f, puissance f*

by main force; by sheer strength — *de vive force*

stretch out: *étendre v*

lying full-length; stretched out full-length — *étendu tout de son long*

strike (a match): s'allumer *v*

to strike a match — frotter une allumette

strike: grève *f*

to go on strike — se mettre en grève

to be on strike — être en grève; faire en grève

strip off: se déshabiller *v*

to strip off — se mettre à poil

strong-minded: résolu *adj*

he is strong-minded — il a la forte tête

strong: fort,-e *adj*

she is still going strong — elle est toujours d'attaque

stumble: trébucher *v*

to stumble; to make a foolish mistake; to make a faux pas — faire un faux pas

stunning: sensationel,-elle *adj*, fantastique *adj*

that's breathtaking; that's stunning — ça décoiffe

stupid: bête *adj*

how can anyone be so stupid! — ce n'est pas possible d'être aussi bête!

how stupid of me!; what a fool I am! — que je suis bête!

to be a stupid fool; to be as thick as a plank — être bête comme ses pieds

style: style *m*

turgid style; pompous style; high-flown style — style ampoulé

stymie, catch out: coincer *v*

I'm stymied — je suis coincé; je suis dans une impasse

succeed: réussir *v*

by dint of trying he succeeded — à force d'essayer, il a réussi

success: succès *m*

to achieve great success — remporter un vif succès

suddenly: brusquement *adv*, soudainement *adv*

point-blank; bluntly; suddenly — de but en blanc

sue: poursuivre *v*

to sue someone for damages — poursuivre quelqu'un en dommages-intérêts

suggestion: *suggestion f*

that's not a bad suggestion (or idea)!   *ce n'est pas bête!*

suit: *arranger v, convenir v à*

that suits me nicely; that's fine by me   *cela m'arrange bien*

sulk: *bouder v*

to flare up; to get huffy; to go off in the sulks   *prendre la mouche*

sulky: *boudeur,-euse adj, maussade adj*

to look sulky   *faire le gueule; faire la tête*

summer: *été m*

in the height of summer   *au cœur de l'été; au plus fort de l'été;*

sun: *soleil m*

at sunset   *au coucher du soleil; à soleil couché*

at sunrise   *au lever du soleil*

sunstroke: *insolation f*

to get sunburnt; to get a touch of sunstroke   *recevoir un coup de soleil*

superior: *supérieur,-e adj*

to be far superior to   *l'emporter de beaucoup sur*

support: *appui m*

in support of this; to back this up   *à l'appui (de)*

suppose: *supposer v*

let's suppose that I am right   *mettons que j'aie raison*

suppose for argument's sake   *supposez pour un instant*

sure (be): *être v sûr*

be sure to come early   *ne manquez pas de venir de bonne heure*

sure: *sûr,-e adj, certain,-e adj*

I am not quite sure what to do   *je ne sais trop que faire*

I am not too sure whether   *je ne sais trop si*

of course; surely   *bien sûr; bien entendu*

surprise: *surprendre v*

to pay a surprise visit to friends   *surprendre des amis chez eux*

surprise: *surprise f*

to pretend to be surprised   *jouer la surprise*

suspicious: *soupçonneux,-euse adj, méfiant,-e adj*

to be uneasy; to be suspicious	*avoir la puce à l'oreille*

swagger: *plastronner v*

to swagger; to strut about	*rouler les mécaniques*

swallow: *avaler v*

he swallowed it in one gulp; he drank it in one go	*il a l'avalé d'un trait; il a l'avalé d'un seul coup*
to swallow a bitter pill; to bite the bullet	*avaler le morceau*
to swallow insults; to be taken in	*avaler des couleuvres*

swear to: *affirmer v*

can you be certain about it?; can you swear to it?	*pouvez-vous l'affirme?*

T

take: *prendre v*

I took you for someone else	*je vous ai pris pour quelqu'un d'autre*
not to take no for an answer	*ne pas rester sur un refus*
take it or leave it	*c'est à prendre ou à laisser*
to take a house on lease	*prendre une maison à bail*
to take a sudden dislike to	*prendre en grippe*
to take flight (bird); to spring into life; to develop rapidly	*prendre son essor*

take aback: *interloquer v*

to be badly let down; to be taken aback	*tomber de haut*

take advantage: *profiter v de*

to turn to good account; to take advantage of	*tirer parti de*

take care not to: *se garder v de*

take care not to make a noise when you go in	*gardez-vous de faire du bruit en entrant*

take in (deceive): *avoir v, rouler v*

he's easily taken in	*il se fait facilement avoir*
to take someone in; to get someone confused	*mettre quelqu'un dedans*

taken aback (to be): être v interloqué

to stand aghast; to be taken aback — *tomber des nues*

take up: reprendre v, aborder v

the problem has been taken up by the manager — *le problème a été repris par le directeur*

talk: causer v, parler v, raconter v

he'll talk your ear off; he's a windbag — *il est bavard comme une pie*

he's talking rubbish (or nonsense) — *il raconte n'importe quoi*

one might as well be talking to a wall — *autant parler à un mur*

to talk business; to talk shop — *parler d'affaires*

to talk fashions; to talk clothes — *parler chiffons*

to talk shop (or politics) — *causer travail (ou politique)*

task: tâche f

he is up to the task — *il est à la hauteur de la tâche*

taste: goût m

tastes differ; there is no accounting for tastes — *à chacun son goût; chacun à son goût*

teach: apprendre v, enseigner v

to teach somebody a lesson; to sort someone out — *apprendre à vivre à quelqu'un*

tears: larmes fpl

to be on the verge of tears — *être sur le point de pleurer*

to burst (or dissolve) into tears — *fondre en larmes*

to have tears in one's eyes — *avoir les larmes aux yeux*

tease: taquiner v

you are teasing me — *tu me taquine*

tell: dire v, raconter v

by the way, tell me — *à propos, dis-moi*

I told you so!; didn't I tell you! — *je vous l'avais bien dit!*

I told you so!; what did I tell you! — *quand je vous le disais!*

tell me; I say — *dis donc; dites donc*

to tell a story; to spin a yarn — *raconter une histoire*

to tell all and sundry; to cry from the rooftops — *annoncer à tous les échos*

to tell someone's fortune	*dire la bonne aventure à quelqu'un*
telly (TV): *télé f*	
turn on the telly (or TV), please	*allume la télé, s'il vous plait*
what's on the telly (or TV) tonight?	*qu'est-ce qu'il y a à la télé ce soir?*
temper: *humeur f, caractère m*	
to be in a foul temper	*être d'une humeur de chien*
to be in a foul temper; to be cantankerous	*être comme un crin*
to be quick-tempered	*avoir la tête près du bonnet*
test: *épreuve f*	
I put him (or it) to the test	*je l'ai mis à l'épreuve*
thanks, thank you: *merci m*	
no thanks, really (or honestly)	*merci, sans façon*
thick-skinned: *peu sensible adj, peu susceptible adj*	
he's very thick-skinned	*c'est un dur, rien ne le touche*
thing: *chose f*	
it's the very thing for me	*ça fait mon beurre*
not to do things by halves	*ne pas faire les choses à demi*
think: *penser v, croire v, dire v, réfléchir v*	
he thinks he's the cat's whiskers	*il se croit sorti de la cuisse de Jupiter; il croit que c'est arrivé*
just imagine!; just think!	*pensez donc!*
no matter what he may think	*quoi qu'il en ait*
one is apt to think that	*on croit volontiers que*
think it over!	*réfléchissez-y!*
to think that	*dire que*
to think twice before doing something	*y regarder à deux fois avant de faire quelque chose*
thinking: *pensée f*	
sound thinking!	*voilà une bonne parole!*
thoroughly: *à fond adv, dans le détail adv*	
thoroughly; in depth	*à fond*
thought: *pensée f, réflexion f*	
on second thoughts	*à la réflexion; réflexion faite*

that's a good one; that's a happy thought	*c'est bien trouvé*
to lose one's train of thought	*perdre le fil*
throw: *jet m*	
it's only a stone's throw from here	*il n'y a qu'un saut d'ici*
throw out: *jeter v dehors*	
throw out; cast aside; get shot of	*mettre au rancart*
thumb: *pouce m*	
at a rough guess; by rule of thumb	*à vue de nez*
to thumb a lift	*lever le (ou faire du) pouce*
to twiddle one's thumbs	*se tourner les pouces*
thunderstruck: *abasourdi,-e adj, ahuri,-e adj*	
I'm thunderstruck; I'm flabbergasted	*les bras m'en tombent*
thus: *ainsi adv*	
just as, as well as	*ainsi que*
tick-off: *attraper v*	
to give someone a good ticking-off	*passer un savon à quelqu'un*
tidy: *ranger v, s'arranger v*	
to tidy up the room	*mettre de l'ordre (ou en ordre) dans la chambre*
time (a long): *longtemps adv*	
I've been working here for a long time	*je travaille ici depuis longtemps*
time: *heure f*	
at any time of the day	*à toute heure*
at this hour (or at such a time) he should be ready for anything	*à pareille heure il devrait être prêt à tout*
at this moment in time	*à l'heure qu'il est; à cette heure*
to have a nasty (or grim) time of it	*passer un sale quart d'heure*
what time do you make it?	*quelle heure avez-vous?*
time: *temps m*	
at that time; in those days	*en ce temps là*

at the proper time; in due time; in due course	*en temps utile; en temps voulu*
at times; from time to time; now and then	*par moments*
at times; now and again; intermittently	*par intervalles*
for the time being; at present	*pour le moment*
for the umpteenth time	*pour la nième fois*
from time to time; now and again	*de temps en temps; de temps à autre*
in his or her spare time	*à (ou dans) ses moments perdus*
in less than no time	*en moins de rien*
in the nick of time; just at the right time	*au bon moment*
it saves a great deal of time; it's very time-saving	*cela fait gagner beaucoup de temps*
off and on; at times	*par instants*
only time will tell	*qui vivra verra*
this comes just at the right time	*cela arrive comme marée en carême*
to arrive in the nick of time	*arriver fort à propos; arriver juste à temps*
to come at just the right time	*tomber à pic (ou à point)*
to have a great time; to have a lot of fun	*s'en payer une tranche*
to have a rough time of it; to have a hard time	*en baver*
to make up for lost time	*rattraper le temps perdu*
with time; in the course of time; as time goes by	*avec le temps; à la longue*
you have just time to; you have just long enough to	*vous avez juste le temps de*
you will have all the time in the world (or all the time you need)	*vous aurez tout votre temps*
tire: *fatiguer v*	
she was not in the least tired	*elle n'était pas le moins du monde fatigué*
to be very fond of: *raffoler v*	
I am passionately fond of music	*je raffole de la musique*

tongue: *langue f*

my mother tongue is French — *ma langue maternelle est française*

top: *dessus m*

to put the best strawberries on top — *mettre les meilleures fraises en dessus*

top: *haut m*

from top to bottom; downwards; high and low — *de haut en bas*

right at the top of a tree — *tout en haut d'un arbre*

toss: *lancement m*

it's a toss-up; it's heads or tails — *c'est à pile ou face*

touch (get in): *contacter v*

to beckon someone; to get in touch with someone — *faire signe à quelqu'un*

touch: *touche f*

to put the finishing touch to — *mettre la dernière main à*

touch: *toucher v*

to have been touch and go; to have a close shave — *revenir de loin*

to touch wood — *toucher du bois*

track: *trace f, piste f*

to be off track; to have missed the point — *mettre à côté de la plaque*

translate: *traduire v*

to translate word for word — *traduire mot à mot*

treat: *traiter v*

to treat some one with disdain; to look down on someone — *traiter quelqu'un de haut en bas*

trendy: *branché,-e adj*

to be trendy — *être dans le vent*

trial: *essai m*

to take someone on a trial basis — *prendre quelqu'un à l'essai*

trick: *ruse f, astuce f, truc m, tour m, niche f*

it's the oldest trick in the book — *c'est le tour classique*

to be up to one's old tricks — *faire des siennes*

to play tricks on someone — *faire des niches à quelqu'un*

trip up: *croc-en-jambe m, croche-pied m*

to trip someone up; to pull a fast one on someone — *donner un croc-en-jambe à quelqu'un*

trouble: *difficulté f, embarras m, ennui m*

there's trouble coming our way! — *ça nous pend au nez*

to get into a mess; to bring trouble on oneself — *s'attirer des ennuis*

to get out of a difficulty; to get out of trouble — *se tirer d'embarras*

to give a great deal of trouble; to have one's work cut out — *donner du fil à retordre*

to go to great trouble to help someone — *se mettre en quatre pour quelqu'un*

to go to great trouble (or bend over backwards) to do something — *se donner un mal de chien à faire quelque chose*

troublemaker: *fauteur m (fautrice f) de troubles*

he's a troublemaker — *il ferait battre des montagnes*

true: *vrai, vraie adj*

it is too good to be true — *c'est trop beau pour être vrai*

it is true nevertheless — *ça ne laisse pas d'être vrai*

quite true!; how right you are! — *tu l'as dit!*

to ring true — *avoir l'accent de la vérité*

trumpet: *trompette f*

to blow one's own trumpet — *s'envoyer des fleurs*

truth: *vérité f, vrai m*

to speak the truth — *dire la vérité*

in actual fact; actually; to tell the truth — *à vrai dire; à dire vrai*

try: *essayer v*

to try on; to try out — *faire l'essai de*

however much I try, I can't do it — *j'ai beau essayer, je n'y arrive pas*

turn: *tourner v*

to turn upside down — *mettre sens dessus dessous*

twig: *piger v, comprendre v*

he didn't twig; he didn't smell a rat — *il n'y a vu que du bleu*

he's twigged; the penny has dropped; he's cottoned on — *il a pigé*

twist (meaning): *déformer v, fausser v*

to twist the truth — *faire une entorse à la vérité*

U

unaware of: *ignorant adj de*

to take (or catch) someone
unawares

*prendre quelqu'un au
dépourvu*

unbelievable: *incroyable adj*

that's unbelievable!; I'd never
have believed it!

on aura tout vu!

underhandedly: *sournoisement adv*

to act underhandedly

agir en dessous

underneath: *en dessous adv*

underneath; in an underhand
manner

en dessous

understand: *comprendre v*

I do not understand; I don't
get it

je n'y suis pas

I don't understand anything
about it

*je ne comprends rien
là-dedans*

is that quite clear?; is that
understood?

c'est bien vu?

of course; understood

bien entendu

you do not understand at all;
you haven't got it at all

tu n'y es pas du tout

unexpected: *inattendu,-e adj*

unexpected event; bolt from the
blue; love at first sight

coup de foudre

unintentionally: *involontairement adv*

I did it unintentionally; I did it
by mistake

je l'ai fait par inadvertance

until: *jusque prep*

how long are you staying?

jusqu'à quand restez-vous?

until now; up to now

jusqu'ici

up till then; until then

jusqu'alors; jusques alors

unwelcome: *importun,-e adj*

to be out of place; to be
unwanted; to be unwelcome

être de trop

upstream: *en amont m*

the bridge is upstream from here

le pont est en amont d'ici

use: *usage m*

to have no use for

n'avoir que faire de

usual: *habituel,-elle adj*

as I usually do — *selon mon habitude*

as usual — *comme d'habitude; comme de coutume*

as usual; usually — *comme d'ordinaire; comme à l'ordinaire*

more/less than usual — *plus/moins que de coutume*

utmost: *le plus possible m*

he does his utmost — *il y va tout son cœur*

I will do my utmost — *je ferai tout mon possible*

de mon mieux

V

vain (in): *en vain adj*

to try in vain — *essayer en vain*

value: *apprécier v*

to value highly; to have a high opinion of — *faire grand cas de*

vanish: *disparaître v*

to vanish into thin air — *disparaître dans la nature*

variance: *désaccord m*

to be at odds (or variance) with — *être en désaccord avec*

view: *vue f*

bird's-eye view — *vue à vol d'oiseau*

from every point of view; in all respects — *à tous égards*

from every point of view; in every respect — *sous tous les rapports*

vigour: *vigueur f, énergie f*

he's full of vigour and won't stop talking — *il est remonté, il n'arrête pas de parler*

VIP: *personnage m de marque*

VIP; Very Important Person; a big shot — *un gros bonnet*

voice: *voix f*

her voice sounds so sweet — *sa voix a un timbre si doux*

to speak in a broken voice — *parler d'une voix entrecoupée*

vote: *voix f, vote m*

to put the question to the vote — *mettre la question aux voix*

W

wait: attendre *v*

I can't wait for the day when that happens	je rêve du jour où cela arrivera
I can't wait to see him again!	je meurs d'envie de le revoir!
that was worth waiting for	cela valait la peine d'attendre
wait for it!	tenez-vous bien!; tiens-toi bien!
we'll just have to wait and see	il va falloir attendre; il va falloir voir venir

walk: marcher *v*, se promener *v*

to go for a walk (or stroll)	faire une promenade ✓
to walk backwards	marcher à reculons
to walk stealthily	marcher à pas de loup
to walk the streets; to wander aimlessly about	battre le pavé
to walk up and down	se promener de long en large
to walk up and down; to walk about	aller et venir
we walked along together	nous avons fait route ensemble

want: manque *m*

for want of something better	faute de mieux

want: vouloir *v*, demander *v*

all I want is to (+vb)	je ne demande qu'à (+inf)

wash: laver *v*

she is washing up	elle lave (ou fait) la vaisselle

washing: lessive *f*

she is doing the washing	elle fait la lessive

watch out: faire *v* le guet

to be on the look-out; to be on the watch	être aux aguets

way (in this): ainsi *adv*

and it is in this way that	et c'est ainsi que
that's the way of the world	ainsi va la monde

way (to get under): démarrer *v*

to get something going (or under way)	mettre quelque chose en train

way: *chemin m, voie f*

come this way	*passez par ici*
not to know which way to turn	*ne plus savoir où donner de la tête*
on the way to recovery	*en voie de guérison*
she returned the same way	*elle est revenue par le même chemin*
they went the wrong way	*ils ont fait fausse route*
to be well on the way to achieving something	*être en chemin de faire quelque chose*

way: *façon f, manière f, moyen m*

in any case; at any rate; anyway	*de toute manière*
in no way; under no circumstances; on any account	*en aucune manière*
in such a way that	*de telle manière que*
somehow or other; in some way or another	*d'une façon ou d'une autre*
there's no way it can be done	*il n'y a pas moyen de moyenner*
to be in a poor way	*être mal en point*
to find a way to	*trouver moyen de (+inf)*
what a way to behave!	*en voilà des manières!*

way of (by): *en guise f de*

by way of thanks	*en guise de remerciement*

wear: *porter v*

to be wearing one's glad rags; to be dressed to kill	*être sur son trente et un*

wear out (person): *épuiser v, pomper v*

to be fagged out; to be bushed	*avoir le coup de pompe*

weather forecast: *météo f*

the weather forecast is good today	*la météo est bonne aujourd'hui*

welcome: *accueil m*

to welcome someone; to make someone welcome	*faire bon accueil à quelqu'un*

well: *bien adv*

I am wonderfully well; I am in excellent health	*je me porte à merveille*
to be well; to be right (clock)	*aller bien*
to get on well together	*faire bon ménage*

would just as soon; be just as well; may as well	*aimer autant*
well: *tiens! excl*	
well, that's how it is my friend	*ma foi, c'est comme ça, mon ami*
well-being: *bien-être m*	
a great feeling of well-being	*un grand sentiment de bien-être*
what: *quoi pron*	
what is it this time?	*quoi encore?*
what is the use? (of doing something)	*à quoi bon? (faire quelque chose)*
what: *que pron*	
what could I say?	*que dire?*
what's to be done?	*que faire?*
whatever: *quel que, quelle que, quoi que adj,adv & pron*	
whatever happens; come what may	*quoi qu'il arrive*
whatever the result, I will do it	*quel que soit le résultat, je le ferai*
whatever we do	*quoi que nous fassions*
where: *où adv & conj*	
where the dickens has he put his shoes?	*où diable a-t-il mis ses chaussures?*
while (little): *moment m, instant m*	
a little while ago; just now; in a little while; shortly	*tout à l'heure*
while: *tant que conj, pendant que conj*	
as long as I live	*tant que je vivrai*
while he rests, she does the housework	*pendant qu'il se repose, elle fait le ménage*
whisper: *chuchoter v*	
she whispers to me	*elle me parle à l'oreille (ou à voix basse)*
white: *blanc adj & m*	
to become as white as a sheet	*devenir blanc comme un linge*
why: *pourquoi adv & conj*	
what(ever) for?	*pourquoi faire?*
why not?	*pourquoi pas?*

   wife: femme *f*

a midwife   *une sage-femme*

   will: volonté *f,* désir *m*

to do something against one's   *faire quelque chose à son*
will   *corps défendant*

   willing (be): être *v* prêt, vouloir *v* bien

to be willing; to be happy   *vouloir bien*

   win: gagner *v*

to hit (or win) the jackpot   *gagner le gros lot*

to win eaily; to win hands down   *gagner haut la main*

to win hands down; to romp   *arriver dans un fauteuil*
home

to win over   *gagner à sa cause*

   wind: vent *m*

he has the wind in his sails   *il a le vent en poupe*

   wise: sage *adj*

to be getting on in years; to be   *prendre de la bouteille**
older and wiser

   without: sans *prep*

he is penniless; he is down   *il est sans le sou; il n'a pas le*
and out   *sou; il est sans ressources*

to be short of; to be without;   *être démuni de*
to be lacking in

   witty remark: mot *m* d'esprit, bon mot *m*

to make witty remarks   *faire des mots*

   woman, man: femme *f,* homme *m*

woman/man of sense; level-   *femme/homme de tête*
headed woman/man

   woman: femme *f*

a prudent woman   *une femme sage*

   wonder: merveille *f,* prodige *m*

to work wonders   *faire des merveilles; faire*
                      des prodiges

   wonder: se demander *v*

I wonder whether   *je me demande si*

   wood: bois *m*

we're not out of the wood yet   *on n'est pas sorti de*
                      l'auberge

word: *mot m, parole f, terme m*

he can't get his words out fast enough	*ça se bouscule au portillon*
in brief; in a few words; in a nutshell	*en abrégé*
in every sense of the word	*dans toute l'acception du mot*
in other words	*en d'autres termes*
in the full sense of the word	*dans toute la force du terme*
just say the word; you've only to say the word	*vous n'avez qu'à parler*
not to be able to get a word in edgeways	*ne pas pouvoir placer un mot*
sharp words; cutting words	*paroles aigres*
to be never at lost for words	*n'être jamais en reste*
to keep one's word; to be as good as one's word	*tenir parole*
to pass by word of mouth; to be rumoured about	*passer de bouche en bouche*
to take somone at his or her word	*prendre quelqu'un au mot*

work: *œuvre f*

to set to work; to get down to work	*se mettre à l'œuvre*

work: *travail m*

he works like a horse	*il travaille comme quatre*
to get down to (hard) work	*aller au charbon*
to get through a lot of work	*battre de la besogne; abattre du travail*
to make short work of (e.g. dish, opponent)	*ne faire qu'une bouchée de (ex. un plat, adversaire)*
to work by fits and starts	*travailler par accès; travailler par à-coups*
to work for nothing; to get nothing out of it	*travailler pour le roi de Prusse*
to work hard	*travailler ferme; travailler dur*

work hard: *travailler v dur*

to be hard at it	*être sur la brèche*

world: *monde m*

I wouldn't do that for anything in the world	*je ne ferais cela pour rien au monde*

it takes all sorts to make a world | *il faut de tout pour faire un monde*

there's a world of difference between the two; they are worlds apart | *il y a un monde entre les deux*

worry: *s'inquiéter* v

don't let it worry you | *t'en fais pas!*

don't worry, everything will be all right | *soyez tranquille, tout ira bien*

to be worried stiff (or to death) | *se faire un sang d'encre*

to get worried; to get worked up | *se mettre martel en tête*

to fret; to worry; to get into a state | *se faire du mauvais sang*

to worry; to worry oneself grey; to fret | *se faire des cheveux*

worry: *souci* m

not a chance!; no fear!; don't you worry | *(il n'y a) pas de danger!*

to be carefree; to have no worries | *être sans souci*

worse: *pire* m, *plus mauvais* adj

that leads one to fear the worse | *ça donne lieu de craindre le pire*

there's worse to come | *on n'a pas vu le pire*

to make matters worse | *pour surcroît de malheur*

worst: *pis* m

at the worst; if the worst comes to the worst | *au pis aller*

to get the worst of it; to come off worst | *avoir le dessous*

to get worse and worse | *aller de pis en pis*

worth (be): *valoir* v

it is not worth while; there is no point in | *ce n'est pas la peine de* (+inf)

it's utterly worthless | *ça ne vaut pas un clou*

it is worth its weight in gold | *il vaut son pesant d'or*

it's worthwhile trying | *cela vaut la peine d'essayer*

to be worth the trouble | *valoir le coup*

write: *écrire v*

to write out in full; to put in black and white	*écrire en toutes lettres*
to write something off	*faire une croix sur quelque chose*

wrong: *mal adj*

he goes the wrong way about it	*il s'y prend mal*
to get on the wrong side of somebody; to get into someone's bad books	*se mettre mal avec quelqu'un*

Y

year: *année f*

he goes fishing all the year round	*il va à la pêche toute l'année*

yours: *les vôtres mpl, fpl*

Happy New Year to you and yours	*bonne année à vous et tous les vôtres*

TOPIC VOCABULARIES

ANIMALS   ANIMAUX

ass	âne *m*
bitch	chienne *f*
bull	taureau *m*
calf	veau *m*
cat	chat *m*, chatte *f*
chicken	poulet *m*; poule *f*
colt	poulain *m*
cow	vache *f*
crossbred (dog)	chien *m* bâtard
dog	chien *m*
donkey	âne *m*
duck	canard *m*; cane *f*
ewe	brebis *f*
filly	pouliche *f*
goat: he-goat	bouc *m*
she-goat	chèvre *f*
goose	oie *f*
greyhound	lévrier *m*
guide dog	chien *m* d'aveugle
gundog	chien *m* de chasse
heifer	génisse *f*
horse	cheval *m*
cart horse	cheval *m* de trait (ou labour)
hack	cheval *m* de louage
race horse	cheval *m* de course
saddle horse	cheval *m* de selle
thoroughbred horse	cheval *m* pur sang
kitten	chaton *m*; petit chat *m*
lamb	agneau *m*
mare	jument *f*
mastiff	mastiff *m*; mâtin *m*
mouse	souris *f*
mule	mulet *m*
ox	bœuf *m*
pedigree dog	chien *m* de race

pointer	chien *m* d'arrêt
pony	poney *m*
pony trekking	randonnée à poney
puppy (dog)	chiot *m*
puppy (dog)	jeune chien(ne) *m,f*
ram	bélier *m*
retriever	chien *m* rapporteur
setter	chien *m* couchant
sheep	mouton *m*
sheepdog	chien *m* de berger
spaniel	épagneul *m*
stallion	étalon *m*
turkey	dinde *f*
water-spaniel	barbet *m*

ART   ART

art	art *m*
abstract art	art *m* abstrait
art deco	art *m* déco
art exhibition	exposition *f* de peinture/ sculpture
art gallery	musée *m* d'art
art school	école *f* des beaux-arts
contemporary art	art *m* contemporain
fine art	les beaux-arts *mpl*
modern art	art *m* moderne
artist; painter	artiste *m, f*; peintre *m*
canvas	toile *f*
colour	couleur *f*
psychedelic colours	couleurs *fpl* psychedeliques
draw	dessiner *v*
drawing	dessin *m*
gouache	gouache *f*
landscape	paysage *m*
literature	littérature *f*
museum, art gallery	musée *m*
still life	nature *f* morte

paint (to)	peindre v
to paint in oils	peindre à l'huile
to paint in water colours	faire de l'aquarelle
paint box	boîte f de couleurs
painting	peinture f, tableau m
painting in oils	peinture f à l'huile
abstract painting	peinture f abstraite
play (theatre)	pièce f
portrait	portrait m
sketch (drawing)	croquis m
sketch book	carnet m à croquis
surrealism	surréalisme m
theatre	théâtre m
in the wings (stage)	dans les coulisses
the house is full (theatre)	la salle est comble
water colour (painting)	aquarelle f
water colour paint	peinture f pour aquarelle

CARDS   CARTES

ace	as m
bridge	bridge m
bid	demande f; annonce f
he bid three diamonds	il demande trois carreaux
pass!; no bid!	parole!; passe!
to pass; to make no bid	passer parole
to raise the bid	relancer
rubber	
that's game and rubber	c'est la partie
to play a rubber	faire un robre; faire une partie
trumps	atout m
two no-trumps	deux sans atout m
call: it's your call	à vous de dire
club(s)	trèfle m
deal	donne f; distribution f
deal (to)	donner (ou distribuer) les cartes
it's your deal	à vous la donne; à vous de donner

diamond(s)	carreau *m*
to show one's hand of cards	abattre *v* son jeu (ou ses cartes)
heart(s)	cœur *m*
jack; knave	valet *m*
joker	joker *m*
king	roi *m*
make a trick	faire un pli
manille	manille *f*
ace (in manille)	manillon *m*
pack of cards	jeu *m* de cartes
patience	patience *f*; réussite *f*
playing cards	cartes *fpl* à jouer
poker	poker *m*
flush	flush *m*; longue couleur *f*; couleur *f*
four of a kind	carré *m*
full house	main *f* pleine; full *m*
high card	carte *f* isolée
one pair	paire *f*
royal flush	quinte *f* royale
straight flush	quinte *f*, séquence *f* flush
three aces	brelan *m* d'as
three of a kind	brelan *m*
two pairs	double paire *f*
pontoon	vingt-et-un *m*
queen	dame *f*
the queen of clubs	la dame de trèfle
run; straight run	séquence *f*
shuffle	
give the cards a good shuffle	bats bien les cartes
to shuffle the cards	battre *v* (ou brasser, ou mêler) les cartes
solitaire	solitaire *m*
spade(s)	pique *m*
suit	couleur *f*
trick	pli *m*, levée *f*
to take a trick	faire un pli, faire une levée
to lose a trick	perdre un pli

trumps	atout *m*
what are trumps?	quel est l'atout *m*?
spades are trumps	atout *m* pique
whist	whist *m*

FAMILY RELATIONS   LA FAMILLE

ancestor	ancêtre *m*
aunt	tante *f*
brother	frère *m*
brother, step-	demi-frère *m*
brother-in-law	beau-frère *m*
children	enfants *m, fpl*
cousin	cousin *m*, cousine *f*
daughter	fille *f*
daughter, adopted	fille *f* adoptive
daughter-in-law; stepdaughter	belle-fille *f*
family tree	arbre *m* généalogique
father-in-law, stepfather	beau-père *m*
first cousin	cousin *m* germain, cousine *f* germaine
foster or adoptive father	père *m* adoptif
foster mother; wet-nurse	mère *f* nourricière
foster or adoptive mother	mère *f* adoptive
grandchild	petit-enfant *m*
granddaughter	petite-fille *f*
grandfather	grand-père *m*
grandmother	grand-mère *f*
grandparents	grands-parents *mpl*
grandson	petit-fils *m*
great-aunt	grand-tante *f*
great-grandfather	arrière-grand-père *m*
great-grandmother	arrière-grand-mère *f*
great-uncle	grand-oncle *m*
half-brother	demi-frère *m*
half-sister	demi-sœur *f*
half-sister, on the father's side	sœur consanguine de père
husband	mari *m*
in-laws	beaux-parents *mpl*

in-laws (generally)	belle-famille *f*
maternal aunt	tante *f* maternelle
maternal uncle	oncle *m* maternel
mother	mère *f*
mother-in-law; stepmother	belle-mère *f*
my relatives	mes parents, ma famille, mes proches
nephew	neveu *m*
next of kin	plus proche parent *m*
niece	nièce *f*
parent	parent *m*
paternal aunt	tante *f* paternelle
paternal uncle	oncle *m* paternel
sister	sœur *f*
sister, step-	demi-sœur *f*
sister-in-law	belle-sœur *f*
son	fils *m*
son, adopted	fils *m* adoptif
son-in-law	beau-fils *m*, gendre *m*
son, step-	beau-fils *m*
spouse	époux *m* (mari); épousse *f* (femme)
uncle	oncle *m*
wife	femme *f*

OCCUPATION   MÉTIER

architect	architecte *m*
artist	artiste *m, f*
chef	chef *m* de cuisine
civil servant	fonctionnaire *m, f*
computer operator	opérateur *m* /opératrice *f* sur ordinateur
cook	cuisinier *m*, cuisinière *f*
dentist	dentiste *m, f*
director (company, programme)	directeur *m*, directrice *f*
doctor	docteur *m*, médecin *m*
engineer	ingénieur *m, f*
estate agent	agent *m* immobilier

flight engineer	mécanicien *m* navigant
hairdresser	coiffeur *m*, coiffeuse *f*
history teacher	professeur *m* d'histoire
lawyer, barrister	avocat *m*, avocate *f*
lawyer	juriste *m*, *f*
manager (bank, theatre etc)	directeur *m*, directrice *f*
manager (shop, workshop etc)	responsable *m*, *f*
manager (restaurant, shop etc)	gerant *m*, gerante *f*
mechanic	mécanicien *m*, mécanicienne *f*
motor mechanic	mécanicien *m* garagiste
musician	musicien *m*, musicienne *f*
notary	notaire *m*
nurse	infirmier *m*, infirmière *f*
nurse (children's)	bonne *f* d'enfants (ou nurse *f*)
pianist	pianiste *m*, *f*
potter	potier *m*, potière *f*
programmer	programmeur *m*, programmeuse *f*
receptionist	réceptionniste *m*, *f*
salesman; representative	réprésentant *m* de commerce
sales manager	chef *m* des ventes
scientist	scientifique *m*, *f*
secretary	secrétaire *m*, *f*
singer	chanteur *m*, chanteuse *f*
medical/arts student	étudiant(e) *m*, *f* en médecine/en lettres
student	étudiant *m*, étudiante *f*
surgeon	chirurgien *m*, chirurgienne *f*
teacher	professeur *m*
teacher	maître *m*/maîtresse *f* d'école
translator	traducteur *m*, traductrice *f*
worker (office)	employé *m* /employée *f* de bureau
worker (factory, agric., etc)	ouvrier *m*, ouvrière *f*

POLITICS LA POLITIQUE

ambassador	ambassadeur *m*
capitalism	capitalisme *m*

communist	communiste *m, f*
Conservative	consevateur *m*, conservatrice *f*
democracy	démocratie *f*
deputy	député *m*
embassy	ambassade *f*
Euro-MP	député *m* au Parlement européen
French Communist Party	Parti *m* communiste français (PCF)
Gaullist Right Party	Rassemblement pour la République (RPR)
the new government	le nouveau gouvernement
to back the government	soutenir *v* le gouvernement
House (Upper/Lower)	Chambre *f* Haute/Basse
Labour	les travaillistes *m, fpl*
Labour Party	Parti *m* travailliste
the Liberals	les libéraux *mpl*
majority vote	scrutin *m* majoritaire
member of parliament	parlementaire *m, f*; député *m* brittanique
minister	ministre *m*
Minister of Education	ministre *m* de l'Éducation
Minister of Agriculture	ministre *m* de l'Agriculture
Minister of Defence	ministre *m* de la Défense
National Front	Front *m* national (FN)
opinion poll	sondage *m* (d'opinion)
the Opposition	l'Opposition *f*
Parliament	Parlement *m*
politician	politicien *m*, politicienne *f*
politician	*LE* politique *m*
polling day	le jour du scrutin *m*
president	président *m*
President of the Senate	le président du Sénat
Prime Minister	Premier ministre *m*
proportional representation	représentation *f* proportionnelle
elected by proportional voting	élus à la proportionnelle
referendum	référendum *m*
Senate	Sénat *m*
senator	sénateur *m*

single currency	monnaie *f* unique
socialism	socialisme *m*
socialist	socialiste *m, f*
socialist party	Parti *m* socialiste (PS)
strike	grève *f*
striker	gréviste *m, f*
trade union	syndicat *m*
unemployment	chômage *m*
voter; elector	électeur *m*, électrice *f*
voting, ballot	scrutin *m*

RELIGION   RELIGION

Allah	Allah *m*
archbishop	archevêque *m*
Bible	Bible *f*
Bible study	étude *f* de la Bible
bishop	évêque *m*
cathedral	cathédrale *f*
catholic	catholique *adj*
christian	chrétien *m*, chrétienne *f*
Christianity	christianisme *m*
Protestant church	temple *m* (protestant)
Catholic church	église *f* (catholique)
God	Dieu *m*
Islam	Islam *m*
Islamic	Islamique *adj*
Islamism	Islamisme *m*
Jesus Christ	Jésus-Christ *m*
jew, jewess	juif *m*, juive *f*
Judaism	judaisme *m*
Koran	Coran *m*
mass	messe *f*
at what time is mass?	à quelle heure commence la messe?
minister	pasteur *m*
Mohammed	Mohammed *m*, Mahomet *m*
mosque	mosquée *f*
muslim; moslem	musulman *m, f*

nun	religieuse *f*
penance	pénitance *f*
Pope	Pape *m*
to pray	prier *v*
prayer	prière *f*
prayer book	livre *m* de messe
priest	prêtre *m*
rabbi	rabbin *m*
service	culte *m*
sin	péché *m*
mortal (original, venial) sin	péché mortel (originel, véniel)
sinner	pécheur *m*, pécheresse *f*
synagogue	synagogue *f*
Vatican	Vatican *m*

SEX SEXE

adolescence	adolescence *f*
AIDS	SIDA *m*
androgen (male sex hormone)	androgène *m*
brothel	maison *f* close; maison *f* de tolérance
chauvinist	chauviniste *adj & m, f*
female	femelle *adj & f*
heterosexual	hétérosexuel,-elle *adj & m, f*
homosexual	homosexuel,-elle *adj & m, f*
male	mâle *adj & m*
male menopause	andropause *f*
marriage	mariage *m*
menopause	ménopause *f*
the pill; contraceptive pill	pilule *f*
to be on the pill	prendre la pilule
to come off the pill	arrêter la pilule
oestrogen (female sex hormone)	œstrogène *m*
pornography	pornographie *f*
prostitute	prostituée *f*, prostitué *m*
prostitution	prostitution *f*
puberty	puberté *f*
rape (to)	violer *v*

rape	viol *m*
sex	sexe *m*
sexist	sexiste *adj & m, f*
sexual abuse	abus *m* sexuel
sexuality	sexualité *f*
sexually transmitted disease	maladie *f* sexuellement transmissible
testosterone (male sex hormone)	testostérone *f*

SPORT SPORT

athletics	athlétisme *m*
badminton	badminton *m*
ball (tennis, golf, cricket)	balle *f*
ball (football, rugby)	ballon *m*
ball (billiards, boules)	boule *f*
basketball	basket-ball *m*; basket *m*
boules	boules *fpl*; pétanque *f*
boxing	boxe *f*
car racing	courses *fpl* d'autos
cricket	cricket *m*
cross-country running (or racing)	cross *m*
cycling	cyclisme *m*
flying/standing start	départ *m* lancé/arrêté
football	football *m*; foot *m*
goal	but *m*
goalkeeper	gardien *m* de but
golf	golf *m*
golfer	golfeur *m*, golfeuse *f*
handball	handball *m*
horse racing; equestrian events	hippisme *m*
horse racing	courses *fpl* de chevaux
horse riding; equitation	équitation *f*
pelota	pelote *f*
rugby	rugby *m*
skating rink	patinoire *f*
ski lift	téléski *m*
skiing	ski *m*

swimming	natation *f*
swimming pool	piscine *f*
tennis: hard-court tennis	tennis *m* sur terre battue
indoor tennis	tennis *m* en salle
lawn tennis	tennis *m* sur gazon
tennis terms:	
advantage	avantage *m*
backhand	revers *m*
backhand volley	volée *f* de revers
ball boy	ramasseur *m* de balles
ball girl	ramasseuse *f* de balles
centre service line	ligne *f* médiane de service
deuce	égalité *f*
be at deuce (to)	être à égalité *f*
fault	faute *f*
forehand drive	coup *m* droit
forehand volley	volée *f* de face
he's/she's a good tennis player	c'est une bonne raquette
linesman	juge *m* de ligne
love all; nothing all	rien partout
love fifteen; fifteen love	rien à quinze; quinze à rien
play a backhand shot (to)	faire un revers
racket press	presse-raquette *m, inv*; presse *f*
receiver	relanceur *m*; relanceuse *f*
serve (to)	servir *v*
server	serveur *m*; serveuse *f*
service	service *m*
tennis ball	balle *f* de tennis
tennis court	court *m*/terrain de tennis
tennis net	filet *m*
tennis racket	raquette *f* de tennis
volley	volée *f*
half-time	mi-temps *f, inv*
umpire	arbitre *m*
volleyball	volley-ball *m*
weightlifting	haltérophilie *f*
to do weightlifting	pousser de la fonte
winner	gagnant *m*, gagnante *f*
to be an easy winner	arriver bon premier

answer, reply

  there's no answer — il n'y a personne

  there's no reply — ça ne répond pas

  when will he be back? — quand sera-t-il de retour?

call — coup *m* de téléphone, coup *m* de fils, appel *m*

  I am calling from England — j'appelle d'Angleterre; je téléphone d'Angleterre

  there's a call for you; you are wanted on the phone — il y a un appel pour vous; on te demande au téléphone

  I want to make a person-to-person call — je voudrais une communication avec préavis

  give him a call about it — demande-le-lui au téléphone

call (to) — appeler *v*

  will you tell him (her) that I called — veuillez lui dire que j'ai appelé

call back (to) — rappeler *v*

  would you ask him/her to call me back — pourriez-vous lui demander de me rappeler

charge

  I want to reverse the charges — je voudrais téléphoner en PCV (paiment contre vérification)

dial the number — composez (ou faites) le numéro

dialling code — indicatif *m* (téléphonique)

dialling tone — tonalité *f*

  I'm not getting the dialling tone — je n'ai pas la tonalité (ou le signal)

directory, telephone — annuaire *m* téléphonique

engaged

  the number's engaged — ce n'est pas libre

extension — poste *m*, interne *m*

extension number — numéro *m* du poste

  I want extension 432 please — je voudrais le poste 432 s'il vous plait

hallo, this is Marie speaking — allô, c'est Marie à l'appareil

hold on, please — ne quittez pas!

line — ligne *f*

  it's a very bad line — la ligne est très mauvaise

the line is engaged	la ligne est occupée
the lines are crossed;	les lignes sont embrouillées
we have a crossed line	
message	
would you take a message, please?	pourriez-vous prendre un message, s'il vous plaît?
number	numéro *m*
you can dial the number direct	vous pouvez obtenir ce numéro par l'automatique
out	
he (she) is out at the moment	il (elle) est absent(e) pour le moment
receiver (or handset)	combiné *m*
lift the receiver (or handset)	décrochez le combiné
replace the receiver (handset)	raccrochez le combiné
ring (to)	sonner *v*
it's ringing now	ça sonne!
speak	
I want to speak to	je désire parler à
telephone	téléphone *m*
to be on the telephone	avoir le téléphone
to telephone	téléphoner *v*
wrong number	faux numéro *m*
I've got the wrong number	je me suis trompé de numéro
to dial a wrong number	faire un faux (ou mauvais) numéro

WEATHER   TEMPS

cloudy	nuageux,-euse *adj*
cloudy weather	temps *m* nuageux
the sky has clouded over	le ciel est couvert de nuages
cold	froid,-e *adj*
it's cold	il fait froid
dark: it's dark	il fait sombre
day: what a beautiful day	quelle belle journée
dusty: it's dusty	il fait de la poussière
fine: do you think it will be a nice day tomorrow?	pensez-vous qu'il fera beau demain?

246

it is fine	il fait beau ✓
fog	brouillard m
it's foggy	il fait du brouillard
freeze (to)	geler v
it's freezing	il gèle
frost	gel m
hail	grêle f
it's hailing	il grêle
hot	chaud,-e adj
isn't it hot (today)!	quelle chaleur!
it's hot	il fait chaud
ice	glace f
lightning	foudre f) la
lightning flash	éclair m
lightning, forked	éclair m en zigzags
lightning, sheet	éclair m en nappes
there's lightning in the distance	il y a des éclairs mpl dans le lointain
rain (to)	pleuvoir v
rain	pluie f
it's raining cats and dogs	il pleut des cordes; il tombe (ou pleut) des hallebardes
it's pouring (down)	il pleut à verse
the rain (the snow) is falling again still more heavily	la pluie (la neige) retombe des plus belle
do you think it's going to rain today?	pensez-vous qi'il pleuvra aujourd'hui?
it's raining	il pleut
snow (to)	neiger v
snow	neige f
it's snowing	il neige
squall	bourrasque f; rafale f
thaw	dégel m
it's thawing	il dégêle
thunder	tonnerre m { le
it thunders	il tonne
thunderstorm	orage m ef fromage
we're going to have a storm	il va y avoir de l'orage
weather	temps m
it's close today	le temps est lourd aujourd'hui

thundery weather	temps d'orage
the weather has turned fine	le temps s'est mis au beau
it's rotten (or lousy) weather	il fait temps de chien!
what terrible weather!	quel sale temps!
in wet weather we stay at home	par temps pluvieux nous restons chez nous
what's the weather like?	quel temps fait-il?
weather forecast	météo *f*
what is the forecast?	quelles sont les prévisions météo?
wind	vent *m*
it's windy	il fait du vent
the wind is very strong (or high)	le vent est très fort

EXCLAMATIONS EXCLAMATIONS

alas!	hélas!
I am afraid not!	hélas non!
I am afraid so!	hélas oui!
what on earth!	que diable!
God bless you!	Dieu vous bénisse!
my godfathers!; by jingo!	mes aïeux!
my goodness!; goodness me!	mon Dieu!
good heavens!	bonté divine!
good heavens!; goodness gracious	grand Dieu!, grands Dieux!
I should think not!	hé non!
all right?	ça va?
I say!	dis donc!
well! (resignedly)	enfin!
well! (relief)	ah bon!
well! (surprise, relief)	eh bien!
well! (surprise)	tiens!
what? (surprise)	hein?

AUXILIARY VERBS

■ **AVOIR** to have

	present-**Participles**-past		**Auxiliary**
	ayant	eu	avoir

	Present	**Imperfect**	**Past Historic**	**Imperative**
j'	ai	avais	eus	
tu	as	avais	eus	aie
il/elle	a	avait	eut	
nous	avons	avions	eûmes	ayons
vous	avez	aviez	eûtes	ayez
ils/elles	ont	avaient	eurent	

	Future	**Conditional**	**Subjunctive**	
			Present	**Imperfect**
j'	aurai	aurais	aie	eusse
tu	auras	aurais	aies	eusses
il/elle	aura	aurait	ait	eût
nous	aurons	aurions	ayons	eussions
vous	aurez	auriez	ayez	eussiez
ils/elles	auront	auraient	aient	eussent

■ **ÊTRE** to be

	present-**Participles**-past		**Auxiliary**
	étant	été	avoir

	Present	**Imperfect**	**Past Historic**	**Imperative**
je	suis	étais	fus	
tu	es	étais	fus	sois
il/elle	est	était	fut	
nous	sommes	étions	fûmes	soyons
vous	êtes	étiez	fûtes	soyez
ils/elles	sont	étaient	furent	

	Future	**Conditional**	**Subjunctive**	
			Present	**Imperfect**
je	serai	serais	sois	fusse
tu	seras	serais	sois	fusses
il/elle	sera	serait	soit	fût
nous	serons	serions	soyons	fussions
vous	serez	seriez	soyez	fussiez
ils/elles	seront	seraient	soient	fussent

SOME FREQUENTLY USED VERBS

■ ALLER to go		present-**Participles**-past		**Auxilary**
		allant	allé	être

	Present	**Imperfect**	**Past Historic**	**Imperative**
je/j'	vais	allais	allai	
tu	vas	allais	allas	va
il/elle	va	allait	alla	
nous	allons	allions	allâmes	allons
vous	allez	alliez	allâtes	allez
ils/elles	vont	allaient	allèrent	

	Future	**Conditional**	**Subjunctive**	
			Present	**Imperfect**
j'	irai	irais	aille	allasse
tu	iras	irais	ailles	allasses
il/elle	ira	irait	aille	allât
nous	irons	irions	allions	allassions
vous	irez	iriez	alliez	allassiez
ils/elles	iront	iraient	aillent	allassent

■ CONNAÎTRE to know		present-**Participles**-past		**Auxilary**
		connaissant	connu	avoir

	Present	**Imperfect**	**Past Historic**	**Imperative**
je	connais	connaissais	connus	
tu	connais	connaissais	connus	connais
il/elle	connaît	connaissait	connut	
nous	connaissons	connaissions	connûmes	connaissons
vous	connaissez	connaissiez	connûtes	connaissez
ils/elles	connaissent	connaissaient	connurent	

	Future	**Conditional**	**Subjunctive**	
			Present	**Imperfect**
je	connaîtrai	connaîtrais	connaisse	connusse
tu	connaîtras	connaîtrais	connaisses	connusses
il/elle	connaîtra	connaîtrait	connaisse	connût
nous	connaîtrons	connaîtrions	connaission	connussions
vous	connaîtrez	connaîtriez	connaissiez	connussiez
ils/elles	connaîtront	connaîtraient	connaissent	connussent

■ DONNER to give	present-**Participles**-past donnant		donné	**Auxilary** avoir
	Present	**Imperfect**	**Past Historic**	**Imperative**
je	donne	donnais	donnai	
tu	donnes	donnais	donnas	donne
il/elle	donne	donnait	donna	
nous	donnons	donnions	donnâmes	donnons
vous	donnez	donniez	donnâtes	donnez
ils/elles	donnent	donnaient	donnèrent	

	Future	**Conditional**	**Subjunctive** **Present**	**Imperfect**
je	donnerai	donnerais	donne	donnasse
tu	donneras	donnerais	donnes	donnasses
il/elle	donnera	donnerait	donne	donnât
nous	donnerons	donnerions	donnions	donnassions
vous	donnerez	donneriez	donniez	donnassiez
ils/elles	donneront	donneraient	donnent	donnassent

■ FAIRE to do, to make	present-**Participles**-past faisant		fait	**Auxilary** avoir
	Present	**Imperfect**	**Past Historic**	**Imperative**
je	fais	faisais	fis	
tu	fais	faisais	fis	fais
il/elle	fait	faisait	fit	
nous	faisons	faisions	fîmes	faisons
vous	faites	faisiez	fîtes	faites
ils/elles	font	faisaient	firent	

	Future	**Conditional**	**Subjunctive** **Present**	**Imperfect**
je	ferai	ferais	fasse	fisse
tu	feras	ferais	fasses	fisses
il/elle	fera	ferait	fasse	fît
nous	ferons	ferions	fassions	fissions
vous	ferez	feriez	fassiez	fissiez
ils/elles	feront	feraient	fassent	fissent

■ FINIR to finish		present-**Participles**-past	**Auxilary**
		finissant	fini	avoir
			Past	
	Present	**Imperfect**	**Historic**	**Imperative**
je	finis	finissais	finis	
tu	finis	finissais	finis	finis
il/elle	finit	finissait	finit	
nous	finissons	finissions	finîmes	finissons
vous	finissez	finissiez	finîtes	finissez
ils/elles	finissent	finissaient	finirent	

	Future	**Conditional**	**Subjunctive**	
			Present	**Imperfect**
je	finirai	finirais	finisse	finisse
tu	finiras	finirais	finisses	finisses
il/elle	finira	finirait	finisse	finît
nous	finirons	finirions	finissions	finissions
vous	finirez	finiriez	finissiez	finissiez
ils/elles	finiront	finiraient	finissent	finissent

■ METTRE to put		present-**Participles**-past	**Auxilary**
		mettant	mis	avoir
			Past	
	Present	**Imperfect**	**Historic**	**Imperative**
je	mets	mettais	mis	
tu	mets	mettais	mis	mets
il/elle	met	mettait	mit	
nous	mettons	mettions	mîmes	mettons
vous	mettez	mettiez	mîtes	mettez
ils/elles	mettent	mettaient	mirent	

	Future	**Conditional**	**Subjunctive**	
			Present	**Imperfect**
je	mettrai	mettrais	mette	misse
tu	mettras	mettrais	mettes	misses
il/elle	mettra	mettrait	mette	mît
nous	mettrons	mettrions	mettions	missions
vous	mettrez	mettriez	mettiez	missiez
ils/elles	mettront	mettraient	mettent	missent

■ POUVOIR to be able to

	present-**Participles**-past		**Auxilary**
	pouvant	pu	avoir
			Past
	Present	**Imperfect**	**Historic**	**Imperative**

	Present	**Imperfect**	**Past Historic**	**Imperative**
je	peux (puis-je)	pouvais	pus	
tu	peux	pouvais	pus	not
il/elle	peut	pouvait	put	used
nous	pouvons	pouvions	pûmes	
vous	pouvez	pouviez	pûtes	
ils/elles	peuvent	pouvaient	purent	

	Future	**Conditional**	**Subjunctive**	
			Present	**Imperfect**
je	pourrai	pourrais	puisse	pusse
tu	pourras	pourrais	puisses	pusses
il/elle	pourra	pourrait	puisse	pût
nous	pourrons	pourrions	puissions	pussions
vous	pourrez	pourriez	puissiez	pussiez
ils/elles	pourront	pourraient	puissent	pussent

■ PRENDRE to take

	present-**Participles**-past		**Auxilary**
	prenant	pris	avoir

	Present	**Imperfect**	**Past Historic**	**Imperative**
je	prends	prenais	pris	
tu	prends	prenais	pris	prends
il/elle	prend	prenait	prit	
nous	prenons	prenions	prîmes	prenons
vous	prenez	preniez	prîtes	prenez
ils/elles	prennent	prenaient	prirent	

	Future	**Conditional**	**Subjunctive**	
			Present	**Imperfect**
je	prendrai	prendrais	prenne	prisse
tu	prendras	prendrais	prennes	prisses
il/elle	prendra	prendrait	prenne	prît
nous	prendrons	prendrions	prenions	prissions
vous	prendrez	prendriez	preniez	prissiez
ils/elles	prendront	prendraient	prennent	prissent

		present-**Participles**-past	**Auxilary**
■ **RECEVOIR** to receive		recevant	reçu avoir

	Present	**Imperfect**	**Past Historic**	**Imperative**
je	reçois	recevais	reçus	
tu	reçois	recevais	reçus	reçois
il/elle	reçoit	recevait	reçut	
nous	recevons	recevions	reçûmes	recevons
vous	recevez	receviez	reçûtes	recevez
ils/elles	reçoivent	recevaient	reçurent	

	Future	**Conditional**	**Subjunctive** Present	Imperfect
je	recevrai	recevrais	reçoive	reçusse
tu	recevras	recevrais	reçoives	reçusses
il/elle	recevra	recevrait	reçoive	reçût
nous	recevrons	recevrions	recevions	reçussions
vous	recevrez	recevriez	receviez	reçussiez
ils/elles	recevront	recevraient	reçoivent	reçussent

		present **Participles**-past	**Auxilary**
■ **SAVOIR** to know		sachant	su avoir

	Present	**Imperfect**	**Past Historic**	**Imperative**
je	sais	savais	sus	
tu	sais	savais	sus	sache
il/elle	sait	savait	sut	
nous	savons	savions	sûmes	sachons
vous	savez	saviez	sûtes	sachez
ils/elles	savent	savaient	surent	

	Future	**Conditional**	**Subjunctive** Present	Imperfect
je	saurai	saurais	sache	susse
tu	sauras	saurais	saches	susses
il/elle	saura	saurait	sache	sût
nous	saurons	saurions	sachions	sussions
vous	saurez	sauriez	sachiez	sussiez
ils/elles	sauront	sauraient	sachent	sussent

■ VENIR to come

	present-**Participles**-past		**Auxilary**
	venant	venu	être

	Present	**Imperfect**	**Past Historic**	**Imperative**
je	viens	venais	vins	
tu	viens	venais	vins	viens
il/elle	vient	venait	vint	
nous	venons	venions	vînmes	venons
vous	venez	veniez	vîntes	venez
ils/elles	viennent	venaient	vinrent	

	Future	**Conditional**	**Subjunctive**	
			Present	**Imperfect**
je	viendrai	viendrais	vienne	vinsse
tu	viendras	viendrais	viennes	vinsses
il/elle	viendra	viendrait	vienne	vînt
nous	viendrons	viendrions	venions	vinssions
vous	viendrez	viendriez	veniez	vinssiez
ils/elles	viendront	viendraient	viennent	vinssent

■ VOULOIR to want, to wish

	present-**Participles**-past		**Auxilary**
	voulant	voulu	avoir

	Present	**Imperfect**	**Past Historic**	**Imperative**
je	veux	voulais	voulus	
tu	veux	voulais	voulus	veuille
il/elle	veut	voulait	voulut	
nous	voulons	voulions	voulûmes	veuillons
vous	voulez	vouliez	voulûtes	veuillez
ils/elles	veulent	voulaient	voulurent	

	Future	**Conditional**	**Subjunctive**	
			Present	**Imperfect**
je	voudrai	voudrais	veuille	voulusse
tu	voudras	voudrais	veuilles	voulusses
il/elle	voudra	voudrait	veuille	voulût
nous	voudrons	voudrions	voulions	voulussions
vous	voudrez	voudriez	vouliez	voulussiez
ils/elles	voudront	voudraient	veuillent	voulussent

FRENCH ALPHABET PRONUNCIATION

(Based on English sounds)

A	ah	H	ahsh	O	oh	V vay
B	bay	I	ee	P	pay	W doobler vay
C	say	J	zhee	Q	kew	X eex
D	day	K	kah	R	ehr	Y ee grehk
E	er	L	ell	S	ess	Z zed
F	eff	M	em	T	tay	
G	zhay	N	en	U	ew	
